Getting the Most Out of Mozart

The Vocal Works

David Hurwitz

AMADEUS
PRESS

Published in 2005 by

Amadeus Press, LLC
512 Newark Pompton Turnpike
Pompton Plains, New Jersey 07444, USA

For sales, please contact

NORTH AMERICA

AMADEUS PRESS, LLC
c/o Hal Leonard Corp.
7777 West Bluemound Road
Milwaukee, Wisconsin 53213, USA
Phone: 800-637-2852
Fax: 414-774-3259

E-mail: orders@amadeuspress.com
Website: www.amadeuspress.com

UNITED KINGDOM AND EUROPE

ROUNDHOUSE PUBLISHING LTD.
Millstone, Limers Lane
Northam, North Devon EX39 2RG, UK
Phone: 01237-474474
Fax: 01237-474474
E-mail: roundhouse.group@ukgateway.net

Printed in Canada

Library of Congress Cataloging-in-Publication Data

Hurwitz, David, 1961–
Getting the most out of Mozart : the vocal works / by David Hurwitz.—
1st paperback ed.
        p. cm. — (Unlocking the masters series ; no. 4)
    Discography: p.
    ISBN 1-57467-106-5
    1. Mozart, Wolfgang Amadeus, 1756–1791. Vocal music. 2. Vocal music—
Analysis, appreciation. I. Title. II. Series.

    MT92.M7H89 2005
    782'.0092—dc22

                                                                      2005007928

Epigraph from *Haydn: Chronicle and Works, Volume II*, by H. C. Robbins Landon, published by Indiana University Press.

Getting the Most Out of Mozart

Unlocking the Masters Series, No. 4

To my cousin Thelma, for her kindness in making her living room sofa available, the better to enjoy numerous memorable musical experiences in Manhattan, including an unforgettable evening in the emergency room of Roosevelt Hospital after an accidental shoulder dislocation in the front row of the grand tier of the Metropolitan Opera House during a performance of Wagner's *The Flying Dutchman*. That was some night of theater!

And to Nate, everyone's favorite uncle, for buying me my very first high-quality turntable at the age of fifteen and then letting me earn enough money working for him over the summer to buy a ton of records to play on it. He knew not what he started.

This book is for both of you, with love.

. . . You ask me for an opera buffa. Most willingly, if you want
to have one of my vocal compositions for yourself alone. But if you
intend to produce it on the stage at Prague, in that case I cannot
comply with your wish, because all of my operas are far too closely
connected with our personal circle (Esterház, in Hungary),
and moreover they would not produce the proper effect, which I
calculated in accordance with the locality. It would be quite another
matter if I were to have the great good fortune to compose a brand
new libretto for your theatre. But even then I should be risking
a good deal, for scarcely any man can brook comparison
with the great Mozart.

If I could only impress on the soul of every friend of music, and on
high personages in particular, how inimitable are Mozart's works,
how profound, how musically intelligent, how extraordinarily
sensitive! (for this is how I understand them, how I feel them)—
why then the nations would vie with each other to possess such
a jewel within their frontiers. Prague should hold him fast—
but should reward him, too; for without this, the history of great
geniuses is sad indeed, and gives but little encouragement to posterity
to further exertions; and unfortunately this is why so many promising
intellects fall by the wayside. It enrages me to think that this
incomparable Mozart is not yet engaged by some imperial or royal
court! Forgive me if I lose my head: but I love the man so dearly.

I am, &c.

Joseph Haydn

—Letter of December 1787 to Franz Roth, Prague

Contents

Introduction

In the first volume of this two-book survey of Mozart's greatest music, I spent a good deal of time talking about his feeling for the voice. It's only fair, then, that in this discussion of the vocal works, I give equal consideration to Mozart's writing for instruments. This may sound strange, but it really isn't. Instrumental music's expressive quality depends on many factors, but perhaps the most important of these is the extent to which composers capture the communicative immediacy typical of music *with* words, through their treatment of melody, harmony, rhythm, dynamics, and texture. When words are present, though, and their meaning clear, the composer's art turns to enhancing the sense of the text being sung by devising the most expressively specific setting possible, relying not just on the above musical qualities but on instrumental color as well.

Mozart understood this very clearly. His sensitivity to the meaning of words—and his ability to capture their sense, refine it, and intensify it musically—was second to none, and that is the reason that much of the following discussion will necessarily focus on the nature of his accompaniments. This approach offers the singular advantage of easy audibility, even on first pass: when Mozart chooses a particular instrumental combination, it is because he expects listeners to notice it, not always consciously, but in the way they feel the music. However, one point needs to be very clear: no matter how involved the discussion becomes regarding Mozart's choice of instruments, I am always talking about *accompaniments,* the musical second-string: the voice always dominates and the words themselves invariably provide the best explanation of their musical treatment.

Also, Mozart was not an opera composer like Wagner, who uses specific themes and motives to represent characters, objects, and ideas. He is never doctrinaire in this respect, for while he does find recurring musical analogues to certain emotions, as you will see, and he always ensures that his characters speak consistently through the music that he gives them, this never becomes a formal or constructive principle in its own right. It might have done so, had Mozart been able to call upon the comparatively huge instrumental resources that Wagner had at his disposal. Even though Mozart used the largest orchestra available to him at any given time, in the final analysis his options were still comparatively limited. To restrict one instrumental timbre to one character or emotional situation would have seriously circumscribed the coloristic variety that constitutes the essence of Mozart's operatic orchestration, and so he never boxed himself into this kind of a musical corner. So you will often hear (for example) clarinets in music expressive of love, sadness, and yearning, but you will also encounter these instruments in other contexts, whether simply to add volume to a full accompaniment or to provide a contrasting sonority.

For a general introduction to Mozart's music, I respectfully refer you back to volume 1 of this series, on the instrumental works. Here, I prefer instead to address more specifically an issue that's particularly relevant in considering his vocal pieces, namely, their widely varying quality. Like most composers of his day, Mozart wrote primarily for the voice. There is a tremendous quantity of such music, much of which is hardly ever played at all, and the proportion of familiar to unfamiliar is far greater in this medium than in the instrumental works, if only because pieces such as operas are so much longer. Unlike the instrumental music, where the forms grow and expand as Mozart matures, one sees exactly the opposite tendency in the vocal works: they become more concentrated and concise. Still, when all is said and done, out of more than twenty operas, oratorios, and theatrical works, only seven are regularly seen in actual performance today. From the dozens of Masses, liturgies, services, and shorter sacred works, Mozart's reputation rests on a mere handful.

The reasons for this phenomenon are not difficult to discern. Vocal music in Mozart's day was hugely dependent on local circumstances: the whims of singers, the expenses of production, the conventions of the church, and the quality, source, and dramatic viability of the words that he was paid to set. If a composer receives a commission to write a large instrumental work, he is not inherently disadvantaged by the fact that the ensemble turns out to be a string quartet rather than a full symphony orchestra. However, if he's asked to compose a three-hour long opera and the libretto is stupid, the singers for whom he's tailoring the music mediocre (or conversely, abnormally gifted), the orchestra understaffed or technically challenged, or any combination of these, then even the greatest musician in successfully adapting to these conditions will likely write uninteresting music, or more significantly, music that will subsequently be perceived as uninteresting because of the evident signs of compromise that it cannot hide.

That said, there's still a vast amount of great Mozart vocal music: arguably the most perfect operas ever written, fabulous individual arias, and sacred music that includes some of his most popular works (whether he actually completed them or not). All of these will be considered here, as will the lesser-known operas and a few other worthy pieces besides. I discuss the great Mozart operas individually, and also survey his early works in the same genre, examine the best of his single arias written (mainly) for concert use, and conclude with the most famous and well-loved religious works. On the accompanying CD, you will find plenty of examples drawn from these pieces, and all of the texts and translations that you need to go with them are included as they come up for consideration.

Unfortunately, that does not mean that this book is self-contained. It presupposes, necessarily, that you will have purchased, or plan to purchase, recordings of at least some of the works being discussed. Even more than with his instrumental output, listening to his vocal music requires a serious investment of time, because in order to get the most out of Mozart's love affair with the human voice, you need to follow the music with the words in hand (at least until you know it well). Sure, you can enjoy the tunes for their own sake, but there's so much more pleasure to be gotten from knowing what all of the shouting is about. So even if the rest of this book speaks about Mozart's strategies as a musician first and foremost, I strongly suggest that you take the time to read the relevant words—all of them.

This means, in opera recordings especially, spending a little time with the entire libretto (most aren't very long). The three great Italian operas to texts by Da Ponte in particular are extremely enjoyable as literature and great fun to read, and beyond that, knowing the dramatic context is critical to appreciating the genius Mozart displays in his musical settings. Even in a story as crazy as *The Magic Flute,* knowing what's said in the dialogue (which you can then skip forever when listening to recordings) offers many insights into the situations and reactions of the characters being illustrated musically. If this sounds too obvious then I apologize, but a lot of years spent listening and observing the listening habits of others have taught me a few things, and one of them is this: never be amazed at the power of even a hard-core music lover's inattention when faced with acres of recitative or dialogue in a foreign language. That's just the way it is.

Otherwise, as with the previous survey of instrumental music, I have tried very hard to focus the discussion on plainly audible facts, firm in my belief that the music will tell you all you need to know if you simply listen closely and sympathetically. To this end, I have also provided complete orchestration lists for every number in the seven great operas, as well as all of the concert arias and the major sacred works. Often, merely knowing who plays what reveals so much about how best to listen, and to see Mozart arranging and contrasting the arias and ensembles within an act, or even an entire work, speaks volumes about what he was trying to achieve (and how he did it).

Putting this book together has turned out to be an endless source of fascination and enjoyment for me, and I truly hope the discoveries that you make within these pages bring you similar pleasure and satisfaction.

Part 1

The Great Operas

Mozart's Operatic Style

At the end of the eighteenth century, there was Italian opera, German opera, and French opera. And then, uncategorizably and regardless of language, there was Mozart. His mature operas defined once and for all the standard to which subsequent generations of composers aspired, and continue to meet the highest expectations of music lovers the world over. Besides a few by Monteverdi, Handel, Gluck, Rameau, and Lully, they are still the oldest works in most opera companies' repertoire, and they show no sign of wear or declining popularity, perhaps due to the most remarkable quality of Mozart's best music: its emotional completeness. If it can be said with some truth that Wagner's characters think but seldom act while Verdi's act but seldom think, then Mozart's do both at the same time.

Oversimplifications such as this are seldom useful if taken too literally, but in Mozart's case, the point that needs stressing is that his greatest operas, the three Italian works to words by Lorenzo Da Ponte, achieve a perfect balance between realistic characterization and dramatic pacing, and they do it in a manner found practically nowhere else. It is impossible to emphasize just how difficult this synthesis is to achieve, because the very nature of opera dictates an unavoidable separation between action and expression, between events that move the plot forward and opportunities for the characters to stand still and communicate their feelings.

No composer can escape this fundamental duality, for the simple reason that *dramatic action* happens in real time while *the musical expression of feelings* inevitably stops the plot dead in its tracks for minutes on end. This is as true of Wagner (despite his often seamless musical continuity) as it is with Handel, where the line of demarcation between *aria* (emotional reaction) and *recitative* (action) could not be more strictly maintained. It therefore makes sense to pay special attention to the ways in which Mozart achieves this particularly successful synthesis.

More than most theatrical forms (except perhaps ballet), opera depends on the listener's suspension of disbelief: in a willingness to accept that it's normal for people to spend large amounts of time singing at or with each other. A good composer entices his audience to accept the inherent artificiality of the happenings on stage by creating music that accurately embodies the dramatic circumstances in which the characters find themselves, and that further fleshes them out by giving them sufficient time to define their thoughts and feelings through the music that they sing. These points may seem obvious, but they are worth mentioning all the same, because no composer was more gifted at characterizing through music than was Mozart.

So despite the claims of scholars and theoreticians, dramatists, stage directors, and even reform-minded composers such as Mozart's older contemporary Christoph Willibald Gluck, opera depends for its success first and foremost on the quality of its music. A great composer can go a long way towards overcoming on strength of musical characterization alone what would otherwise be a debilitating silliness of plot, dramatic structure, or circumstance of performance. Mozart understood this fact as well as anyone ever has. Virtually all of his operas contain excellent music specific to both character and the emotional needs of the moment, even in those instances when, saddled with a less-than-stageworthy text, "the moment" lacks dramatic focus or logic (as happens in some of his less successful efforts).

The principal agent of musical characterization in opera is the aria, or song, in which the orchestra accompanies the singer (or singers in the case of duets, trios, quartets, or larger ensembles). Action that advances the plot occurs in the recitatives, of which there are two types. *Secco,* or "dry," recitative (in Mozart's day called "simple" recitative) is basically sung speech lightly accompanied by a keyboard instrument (harpsichord or piano), sometimes with low strings on the bass line. Accompanied recitative, on the other hand, in which the orchestra participates, lies somewhere between the natural speech-rhythms of dry recitative and the more lyrical expression typical of an aria.

One of the principal ways in which Mozart differs from his contemporaries concerns the proportion of time spent in arias as opposed to recitatives. Consider the following table, which compares the relative dimensions between Mozart's *Così fan tutte* and his contemporary Vicente Martin y Soler's *La capricciosa corretta* (chosen at random).

Mozart *Così fan tutte*	Timings (minutes)	Martin y Soler *La capricciosa corretta*
180	Total Time	135
48	Total Recitative	67
67	Act 1: Music Only	26
65	Act 2: Music Only	42
132	Total Music	68
73%	% Music/Total Time	50%
3:1	Ratio—Music:Recitative	1:1
18	Act 1 Finale	5
22	Act 2 Finale	11
40	Total Continuous Music (Finales)	16
31	Total Numbers	31
4.26	Average Length/Number	2.19

Comparison of these two works is striking. Both have two acts containing thirty-one numbers. Both have librettos by Da Ponte concerning the foibles of women. Martin y Soler's work dates from 1795 (some half a decade later than the Mozart) and even acquired as an "insert" an aria from one of Mozart's operas (not as unusual an occurrence as it sounds today). But the differences are even more striking. Martin y Soler's opera consists of 50 percent simple recitative, while with Mozart, the percentage of simple recitative as compared to arias, ensembles, and accompanied recitative (what I call here simply "music") is much smaller—only 27 percent. The amount of continuous music in the big finales is far greater in Mozart, and the average length of each number is longer too, which allows more time for characterization and expression, and means that the mechanics of the plot are reduced to a bare minimum.

The above statistics, however, offer merely a quantitative measure and say nothing about the relative quality of the music itself. So I will now take one typical example of a Mozart aria and consider what it reveals about his gift for creating realistic and emotionally touching characters through the material that they sing. The aria is "Porgi amor" from *The Marriage of Figaro,* and you can find it on track 1 on the companion CD. It represents the audience's first encounter with the Countess, arguably the most sympathetic and important person in the whole opera. She has not appeared at all in act 1. Mozart and Da Ponte have given her solo billing at the opening of act 2, and in less than four minutes of music, they reveal everything that we need to know about her character so that we understand perfectly her motivations and subsequent behavior.

Porgi, amor, qualche ristoro	Love, offer some relief
Al mio duolo, a'meie sospir:	To my sorrow, to my sighs:
O mi rendi il mio tesoro,	O return to me my dearest,
O mi lascia almen morir.	Or I beg you, let me die.

Mozart scores this aria for strings, with pairs of clarinets, bassoons, and horns. No flutes lighten the texture, and no oboes inject their touch of tonal vinegar into the smooth and silky yet melancholy atmosphere created by the orchestral introduction. The Countess sings the entire text twice in order, then repeats the last two lines by way of conclusion. Aside from the sheer loveliness of the melodic line throughout, here are some points that you might want to note when listening:

1. The clarinets don't just accompany the singer, but amplify, extend, and comment upon the vocal line like a sympathetic chorus, immeasurably enhancing the poignancy of the music.
2. At the first appearance of the words "to my sorrow," Mozart provides a thrilling sequence of descending accompanying chords that add depth and intensity to the sorrow being described, but without disturbing the long, lyrical line of the melody.
3. Mozart creates the aria's dynamic climax by having the Countess repeat the most telling words immediately: "let me die," with a big crescendo at the repetition.
4. Notice also the gentle instrumental stab of pain (in the form of a sudden touch of dissonance from the winds) at the words "to my sighs" when they come around for the second time.

So in the course of this brief aria, Mozart gives special emphasis to all of the most highly charged bits of text, to the ideas of sorrow, sighing, and the yearning for death. And yet the music isn't at all depressing, and the big crescendo at "let me die" is immediately reigned in. For all her sadness, the music says, the Countess is a woman of great dignity and self-control who, despite the pain she feels, has not yet given in to self-pity or despair. She still loves her husband, and the sweetness of the vocal line lets the audience know not just the love that she still harbors but what a treasure her husband has so foolishly cast aside. The music simultaneously expresses the Countess's feelings while arousing the listener's sympathy, and from this point on, the audience is squarely on her side.

It's worth pointing out in this connection, then, that although Mozart's operas may be thought of as comparatively long (as compared, for example, to the Martin y Soler), they contain, as Mozart himself is purported to have said, "only as many notes as are necessary." The length is a function of their emotional comprehensiveness, of the need to create three-dimensional characters, but Mozart achieves this goal with really astonishing accuracy and concision. In short, he gives his listeners more bang for their buck than just about anyone else in the business.

This last point raises the final issue demanding consideration in defining the special qualities of Mozartean opera: dramatic pacing. After all, shouldn't the superabundance of music that theoretically stops the plot dead in its tracks render these works boring and dramatically inert? The answer is no, and there are several reasons for it. First, there is the matter of the listener's expectations. Having made the leap of faith required to accept a scenario in which characters stand around and sing at each other, any sympathetic member of the audience, practically speaking, is prepared to be consistently entertained and instinctively bridles (or passes out) if the piece turns out to be boring. All great music has one quality above all else: it grabs and holds the listener's attention.

Second, despite the fact that the plot largely happens in the dry (simple) recitatives, nothing in the universe is duller musically than excessive quantities of this sort of ongoing notated chatter. So when the orchestra starts up and the singers cut loose and strut their stuff, it always comes as a positive relief and an increase in excitement and dramatic tension, even though nothing significant may be happening in terms of action or interaction between the characters—further proof of the primacy of musical considerations above all else. This explains why an opera such as Martin y Soler's *La capricciosa corretta,* with its acres of dry recitative and short, peppy, but emotionally generic arias, is such a bore compared to just about anything by Mozart—even though it may be shorter in absolute length.

Third, and perhaps most importantly, Mozart was the first composer in history to write extensive and effective "action music," which accompanies his characters in real time even as it remains expressively fulfilling. It's impossible to overestimate the significance of this innovation, which had an incalculable impact on virtually all later composers of opera. There are two principal places where you will notice Mozart's action music at work most prominently: right after the overture and in the big finales at the ends of acts. Many of the ensemble pieces, particularly midact duets and trios, also move the plot smartly along at an unobtrusively natural pace.

Another important observation: all four of Mozart's greatest operas, *The Marriage of Figaro, Don Giovanni, Così fan tutte,* and *The Magic Flute,* begin in midstream, as if picking up a story that has already begun. In *Figaro,* the principal character is in the midst of measuring his room for a new bed. In *Don Giovanni,* the servant Leporello is pacing back and forth and complaining, while awaiting his boss's return from a seduction currently in progress. *Così* opens in the middle of an argument between friends about the faithfulness of women. As for *The Magic Flute,* the story begins more in the thick of things than any of the others, with Tamino being chased by a giant serpent. Mozart takes great pains to plunge his audience directly into each situation and, more importantly, creates music that defines the dramatic ambience immediately.

What makes these openings so interesting, particularly when heard directly after the overtures that precede them, is Mozart's understanding of the fact that action music, no matter how exciting, if it is not to sound merely cartoonish, needs to move at the same tempo that people do, and this often means at a speed that is perceived subjectively as slower than that of the overture. Compare, for example, on tracks 2 through 7 of the companion CD, the deliciously frantic overture to *Così fan tutte* (which is the absolute embodiment of gossip in music) with the dashing opening scene among the three male principals (don't worry about the words: just get a feel for the pace of the music). The tempos of both are quick, but the bantering woodwinds, trumpet and drum explosions, and merry-go-round melodic arabesques of the overture fly by like rumors borne on the wind, while the opening trio between the three singers follows a completely natural and believable pattern of exchange between them despite its clear formal and melodic organization. Here's how the entire opening scene, which has five parts, lays out:

1. Trio: Ferrando and Guglielmo protest against Don Alfonso's prior claim that all women, including their girlfriends, are inherently fickle. The conversation thus starts in midstride; it has been going on since before the curtain went up.

2. Dry Recitative: The two young men challenge Don Alfonso to a duel to protest his dishonorable words, and he mockingly refuses them.

3. Trio: Don Alfonso explains his philosophy. Women's virtue is like the Phoenix—everyone believes that it exists, but no one has ever seen it. Ferrando and Guglielmo insist that their girlfriends are goddesses.

4. Dry Recitative: Don Alfonso suggests a wager that he can prove the truth of his assertions, and his companions accept gleefully.

5. Trio: Both sides of the debate celebrate impending victory, each sure that they will win the bet.

This entire scene lasts only about seven to eight minutes. Its most interesting aspect stems not just from the easy and rapid alternation of recitative and ensemble, but also from the way that Mozart expands the musical quotient as the argument proceeds, saving the longest section for last. You will see this same principle at work quite frequently in many of his best operatic scenes. The final trio, which lasts approximately two and a quarter minutes, also includes trumpets and drums to provide the grandest orchestration, thus creating a satisfying climax to the entire opening scene from a purely musical point of view without ever impeding the basic, conversational flow established at the very beginning.

The ability to create music that moves at a realistic human pace and rhythm partly accounts (along with the issue of completeness of characterization) for the extra length of Mozart's operas when compared to those of some of his more popular contemporaries, but it also explains why this is never boring. Mozart's finales offer the most eloquent demonstration of this fact. As the table shows, in *Così,* nearly one third of the total amount of music that is not recitative consists of the two finales. That's forty minutes of continuous music in all, longer than most symphonies or concertos of Mozart's day, and essentially equal in length to any operatic scene by any later composer, including the famously leisurely Wagner. The difference is that Wagner's longest scenes tend to be static monologues or duets (such as *Tristan*'s act 3 "mad" scene or the love scene in the preceding act of that opera), whereas Mozart's finales contain a potent mixture of action and expression in equal measure.

In order to hear how Mozart achieves this miraculous synthesis in real time on the largest possible scale, you will find on track 8 of the accompanying CD the entire act 2 finale (approximately twenty minutes of music) from *The Marriage of Figaro,* with the text and translation printed on the following pages.

First I will briefly set the scene: The Count, who lusts after everything in a skirt, is furious with the young page Cherubino for precisely the same vice and so sends him off to the army. Before he goes, however, Cherubino gets enlisted in Figaro's plot to humiliate the Count (who has for this purpose been given a letter suggesting that the Countess is having an affair). As the scene opens, the suspicious Count believes he has caught the page in his wife's bedroom closet, and that Cherubino is in fact the Countess's lover. Unbeknownst to the two aristocrats, Cherubino has in fact just jumped out of the window and made his escape with the aid of Susanna, Figaro's fiancée, who has taken his place in the closet. Simply follow the words along with the music. My own brief comments are in italics.

Finale

Tempo: allegro (quick)
Orchestration: pairs of oboes, clarinets, bassoons, horns, and strings.

IL CONTE:
[alla porta del gabinetto]
Esci omai, garzon malnato,

sciagurato, non tardar.

LA CONTESSA (ROSINA):
Ah, signore, quel furore
per lui fammi il cor tremar.

IL CONTE:
E d'opporvi ancor osate?

LA CONTESSA:
No, sentite . . .

Finale

COUNT:
[at the door of the closet]
Come out of there, you worthless boy,
miserable wretch, don't delay.

COUNTESS (ROSINA):
Ah, my lord, such a fury
makes my heart tremble for him.

COUNT:
And still you dare to interfere?

COUNTESS:
No, listen . . .

IL CONTE:	COUNT:
Via parlate.	Go on, speak.

LA CONTESSA:	COUNTESS:
Giuro al ciel ch'ogni sospetto . . .	I swear to heaven that every suspicion . . .
e lo stato in che il trovate . . .	and the state in which you find him . . .
sciolto il collo . . .	his collar open . . .
nudo il petto . . .	his chest exposed . . .

IL CONTE:	COUNT:
Sciolto il collo!	His collar open!
Nudo il petto! Seguitate!	His chest exposed! Continue!

The voices increasingly overlap as the argument becomes more intense.

LA CONTESSA:	COUNTESS:
Per vestir femminee spoglie . . .	To get dressed like a woman . . .

IL CONTE:	COUNT:
Ah comprendo, indegna moglie,	Oh, I understand, unworthy wife,
mi vo' tosto vendicar.	I'll avenge myself now.

LA CONTESSA:	COUNTESS:
Mi fa torto quel trasporto,	This fury wrongs me,
m'oltraggiate a dubitar.	Your doubt offends me.

The harmony takes an ominous turn as the Count imagines being dishonored, and also imagines the death of Cherubino, leading quickly back to the music of the above argument.

IL CONTE:	COUNT:
Qua la chiave!	The key!

LA CONTESSA:	COUNTESS:
Egli è innocente.	He's innocent.
[dandogli la chiave]	[gives him the key]
Voi sapete . . .	You know . . .

IL CONTE:
Non so niente.
Va lontan dagl'occhi miei,
un'infida, un'empia sei
e mi cerchi d'infamar.

COUNT:
Don't say anything.
Go far from my sight,
a cruel deceiver, you are,
and you're trying to dishonor me.

LA CONTESSA:
Vado . . . sì . . . ma . . .

COUNTESS:
I'm going, yes, but . . .

IL CONTE:
Non ascolto.

COUNT:
I won't listen.

LA CONTESSA:
Non son rea.

COUNTESS:
I'm not guilty.

IL CONTE:
Vel leggo in volto!
Mora, mora, e più non sia,

ria cagion del mio penar.

COUNT:
I read it in your face!
He dies, dies, and then no longer
will be
the cause of my aggravation.

LA CONTESSA:
Ah, la cieca gelosia
qualche eccesso gli fa far.

COUNTESS:
Ah, blind jealousy
goads him to such excesses.

[Il Conte apre il gabinetto e
Susanna esce sulla porta, ed ivi
si ferma.]

[The Count opens the door
of the closet, and Susanna
comes through the door.]

IL CONTE:
Susanna!

COUNT:
Susanna!

LA CONTESSA:
Susanna!

COUNTESS:
Susanna!

Tempo: molto andante (very moderately). A graceful minuet as Susanna enters, all feigned innocence.

SUSANNA:
Signore,

SUSANNA:
My lord,

cos'è quel stupore?	What is this confusion?
Il brando prendete,	You take your sword,
il paggio uccidete,	you kill the page,
quel paggio malnato,	you see that same worthless boy
vedetelo qua.	before you here.

The three voices overlap in a very brief triple-aside to the audience.

IL CONTE:
(Che scola! La testa
girando mi va.)

COUNT:
(What a shock!
My head is spinning.)

LA CONTESSA:
(Che storia è mai questa,
Susanna v'è là.)

COUNTESS:
(What a story this is,
Susanna was in there.)

SUSANNA:
(Confusa han la testa,
non san come va.)

SUSANNA:
(They're completely stumped,
they don't know what is
happening.)

The musical dialogue resumes.

IL CONTE:
Sei sola?

COUNT:
Are you alone?

SUSANNA:
Guardate,
qui ascoso sarà.

SUSANNA:
You can check,
and you will see for yourself.

IL CONTE:
Guardiamo, qui ascoso sarà.
[entra nel gabinetto]

COUNT:
I'll check and see for myself.
[enters the closet]

Tempo: allegro
Mozart adds flutes to the orchestration to brighten the texture.

LA CONTESSA:
Susanna, son morta,
il fiato mi manca.

COUNTESS:
Susanna, I'm dying,
I'm breathless.

SUSANNA:
[addita alla Contessa la finestra
onde è saltato Cherubino]
Più lieta, più franca,
in salvo è di già.

IL CONTE:
[esce dal gabinetto]
Che sbaglio mai presi!
Appena lo credo;
se a torto v'offesi
perdono vi chiedo;
ma far burla simile
è poi crudeltà.

SUSANNA:
[points to the window from which
Cherubino jumped]
Not to worry,
he's run off to safety.

COUNT:
[exiting the closet]
What a mistake I have made!
I can scarcely believe it;
if I offended you
I beg your pardon;
but to play games in such a fashion
is too cruel.

The following little motive is the ultimate musical equivalent of finger-wagging, and it stays associated with Susanna for the next few minutes:

LA CONTESSA & SUSANNA:
Le vostre follie
non mertan pietà.

IL CONTE:
Io v'amo.

LA CONTESSA:
Nol dite!

IL CONTE:
Vel giuro.

LA CONTESSA:
Mentite.
Son l'empia, l'infida
che ognora v'inganna.

IL CONTE:
Quell'ira, Susanna,
m'aita a calmar.

COUNTESS & SUSANNA:
Your foolishness
doesn't deserve mercy.

COUNT:
I love you.

COUNTESS:
Don't say it!

COUNT:
I swear.

COUNTESS:
You lie.
I'm the mean, faithless one
who forever deceives you.

COUNT:
Such fury, Susanna,
help me calm her.

SUSANNA:
Così si condanna
chi può sospettar.

LA CONTESSA:
Adunque la fede
d'un'anima amante
sì fiera mercede
doveva sperar?
[quasi piangendo]

IL CONTE:
Quell'ira, Susanna,
m'aita a calmar.

SUSANNA:
Così si condanna
chi può sospettar.
[consolando a Contessa]
Signora!

IL CONTE:
Rosina!

SUSANNA:
Thus are condemned
those who are suspicious.

COUNTESS:
So the faithfulness
of a lover's soul
merits only
this cruel reward?
[almost crying]

COUNT:
Such fury, Susanna,
help me calm her.

SUSANNA:
Thus are condemned
those who are suspicious.
[comforting the Countess]
My lady!

COUNT:
Rosina!

Now it's the Countess's turn to be angry.

LA CONTESSA:
[al Conte]
Crudele!
Più quella non sono;
ma il misero oggetto
del vostro abbandono
che avete diletto
di far disperar.

COUNTESS:
[to the Count]
Cruel man!
I am no longer she;
but the miserable victim
of your abandonment
whose pain you caused
for your own delight.

The following three lines are sung together:

IL CONTE:
Confuso, pentito,

COUNT:
I'm confused, I'm sorry,

son troppo punito,
abbiate pietà.

SUSANNA:
Confuso, pentito,
è troppo punito,
abbiate pietà.

LA CONTESSA:
Soffrir sì gran torto
quest'alma non sa.

IL CONTE:
Ma il paggio rinchiuso?

LA CONTESSA:
Fu sol per provarvi.

IL CONTE:
Ma i tremiti, i palpiti?

LA CONTESSA:
Fu sol per burlarvi.

IL CONTE:
Ma un foglio sì barbaro?

SUSANNA:
He's confused, he's sorry,
he's been punished too much,
have pity.

COUNTESS:
This soul doesn't know
how to suffer such wrongs.

COUNT:
But the page locked in there?

COUNTESS:
It was solely to test you.

COUNT:
But your tremors and palpita-
tions?

COUNTESS:
It was only to joke with you.

COUNT:
But that appalling letter?

I've been punished too much,
have pity.

More finger-wagging, not without a touch of malice.

LA CONTESSA & SUSANNA:
Di Figaro è il foglio,
e a voi per Basilio.

IL CONTE:
Ah perfidi! Io voglio . . .

LA CONTESSA & SUSANNA:
Perdono non merta
chi agli altri nol da.

COUNTESS & SUSANNA:
Figaro wrote the letter,
and sent to you through Basilio.

COUNT:
Ah traitors! I want to . . .

COUNTESS & SUSANNA:
One who won't grant pity to
others does not deserve it himself.

IL CONTE:
Ebben, se vi piace
comune è la pace;
Rosina inflessibile
con me non sarà.

COUNT:
Well, if it pleases you
let's have peace;
Rosina wouldn't
be so inflexible with me.

LA CONTESSA:
Ah quanto, Susanna,
son dolce di core!
Di donne al furore
chi più crederà?

COUNTESS:
Ah, Susanna,
how sweet my heart is!
Who will believe any more
in a woman's fury?

SUSANNA:
Cogl'uomin, signora,
girate, volgete,
vedrete che ognora
si cade poi là.

SUSANNA:
With men, my lady,
you twist and you turn,
but you'll see that
we fail there every time.

IL CONTE:
Guardatemi...

COUNT:
Look at me...

LA CONTESSA:
Ingrato!

COUNTESS:
Ungrateful man!

IL CONTE:
Ho torto, e mi pento.

COUNT:
I'm wrong, and I'm sorry.

LA CONTESSA, SUSANNA
& IL CONTE:
Da questo momento
quest'alma a conoscermi/
conoscerla/conoscervi
apprender potrà.

COUNTESS, SUSANNA
& COUNT:
From this moment onwards,
this soul will know
how to understand me/her/you.

Tempo: still quick, but now in the minuet rhythm of Susanna's entrance (although more lively), placing the two servants (and lovers) in the same musical world and also, with the change to triple time, adding an additional jolt of energy. The clarinets drop out, giving the wind writing a harder and more rustic character as well.

FIGARO:
Signori, di fuori
son già i suonatori.
Le trombe sentite,
i pifferi udite,
tra canti, tra balli
de' nostri vassalli
corriamo, voliamo
le nozze a compir.
[prendendo Susanna sotto
il braccio]

FIGARO:
My lord and lady,
the musicians are already outside.
You hear the trumpets,
and the pipes,
with that singing and dancing
of our subjects
let's run, let's fly
to start the wedding.
[takes Susanna by the arm]

IL CONTE:
Pian piano, men fretta;

COUNT:
Wait a minute, don't rush;

FIGARO:
La turba m'aspetta.

FIGARO:
The crowd is waiting for me.

IL CONTE:
Un dubbio toglietemi
in pria di partir.

COUNT:
Just clarify one question for me
before you go.

LA CONTESSA, SUSANNA
& FIGARO:
La cosa è scabrosa;
com'ha da finir!

COUNTESS, SUSANNA
& FIGARO:
This business is frightful;
how will it end!

IL CONTE:
(Con arte le carte
convien qui scoprir.)
[a Figaro]

COUNT:
(This hand must be played
cleverly)
[to Figaro]

Tempo: andante (walking tempo). The Count believes himself to be very sly, and the music backs him up with its moderate pace and casual demeanor. Notice how everyone is basically on the same page at this point except Figaro—so the Count, Countess, and Susanna repeat identical questions to identical music. It's three against one. All of them want Figaro to admit that he knows about the letter, but of course he refuses since he doesn't know that the two women have already spilled the beans.

Conoscete, signor Figaro,
[mostrandogli il foglio]
questo foglio chi vergò?

Do you know, signor Figaro,
[showing him the letter]
who wrote this letter?

FIGARO:
Nol conosco . . .

FIGARO:
I don't know about it . . .

SUSANNA, LA CONTESSA
& IL CONTE:
Nol conosci?

SUSANNA, COUNTESS
& COUNT:
You don't know about it?

FIGARO:
No, no, no!

FIGARO:
No, no, no!

SUSANNA:
E nol desti a Don Basilio . . .

SUSANNA:
And you never gave it to Basilio . . .

LA CONTESSA:
Per recarlo . . .

COUNTESS:
To give to him . . .

IL CONTE:
Tu c'intendi . . .

COUNT:
You see where this is going . . .

FIGARO:
Oibò, oibò.

FIGARO:
Not exactly.

SUSANNA:
E non sai del damerino . . .

SUSANNA:
And you don't know about that
little man . . .

LA CONTESSA:
Che stasera nel giardino . . .

COUNTESS:
Who tonight, in the garden . . .

IL CONTE:
Già capisci . . .

COUNT:
Understand now?

FIGARO:
Io non lo so.

IL CONTE:
Cerchi invan difesa e scusa

il tuo ceffo già t'accusa,
vedo ben che vuoi mentir.

FIGARO:
Mente il ceffo, io già non mento.

LA CONTESSA & SUSANNA:
Il talento aguzzi invano
palesato abbiam l'arcano,
non v'è nulla da ridir.

IL CONTE:
Che rispondi?

FIGARO:
Niente, niente.

IL CONTE:
Dunque accordi?

FIGARO:
Non accordo.

SUSANNA & LA CONTESSA:
Eh via, chetati, balordo,
la burletta ha da finir.

FIGARO:
Per finirla lietamente
e all'usanza teatrale
un'azion matrimoniale
le faremo ora seguir.

FIGARO:
No, I don't.

COUNT:
You search vainly for evasions and
excuses
but your face already accuses you,
I see well that you want to lie.

FIGARO:
Then my face is lying: I'm not
lying.

COUNTESS & SUSANNA:
All your talent has been wasted
we have revealed the secret,
there's nothing more to discuss.

COUNT:
What do you say to that?

FIGARO:
Nothing, nothing.

COUNT:
Then you accept it?

FIGARO:
No, I don't agree.

SUSANNA & COUNTESS:
Be quiet, you fool,
the comedy is finished.

FIGARO:
Then, to end it properly and in
keeping with theatrical tradition
we can now get on with
our wedding ceremony.

LA CONTESSA, SUSANNA
& FIGARO:
[al Conte]
Deh signor, nol contrastate,
consolate i lor/miei desir.

COUNTESS, SUSANNA
& FIGARO:
[to the Count]
My lord, don't forestall them/us,
fulfill their/my wishes.

IL CONTE:
(Marcellina, Marcellina!
Quanto tardi a comparir!)

COUNT:
(Marcellina, Marcellina! How
late you are in getting started!)

Tempo: allegro molto (very quick)

ANTONIO:
Ah, signor . . . signor . . .

ANTONIO:
Oh, my lord . . . my lord . . .

IL CONTE:
Cosa è stato? . . .

COUNT:
What's the matter? . . .

ANTONIO:
Che insolenza! Chi'l fece! Chi fu!

ANTONIO:
What insolence! Who did it!
Who was it!

LA CONTESSA, SUSANNA,
IL CONTE & FIGARO:
Cosa dici, cos'hai, cosa è nato?

COUNTESS, SUSANNA,
COUNT & FIGARO:
What are you saying, what is it,
what's going on?

ANTONIO:
Ascoltate . . .

ANTONIO:
Listen . . .

LA CONTESSA, SUSANNA,
IL CONTE & FIGARO:
Via, parla, di', su.

COUNTESS, SUSANNA,
COUNT & FIGARO:
Go on, speak, tell us.

ANTONIO:
Dal balcone che guarda in giardino
the mille cose ogni dì gittar veggio,

ANTONIO:
From the balcony that looks over
garden I see a thousand things
thrown out constantly,

e poc'anzi, può darsi di peggio,
vidi un uom, signor mio, gittar giù.

and today, even worse than usual,
I saw a man, my lord, thrown out.

IL CONTE:
Dal balcone?

COUNT:
From the balcony?

ANTONIO:
[mostrandogli il vaso]
Vedete i garofani?

ANTONIO:
[showing him the pot]
See my carnations?

IL CONTE:
In giardino?

COUNT:
In the garden?

ANTONIO:
Sì!

ANTONIO:
Yes!

SUSANNA & LA CONTESSA:
[piano a Figaro]
Figaro, all'erta.

SUSANNA & COUNTESS:
[quietly to Figaro]
Figaro, watch out.

IL CONTE:
Cosa sento!

COUNT:
What do I hear!

SUSANNA, LA CONTESSA
& FIGARO:
Costui ci sconcerta,
quel briaco che viene far qui?

SUSANNA, COUNTESS
& FIGARO:
This looks like trouble,
why has that old drunk come here?

IL CONTE:
[ad Antonio]
Dunque un uom . . . ma dov'è,
dov'è gito?

COUNT:
[to Antonio]
So a man . . . but where,
where did he land?

ANTONIO:
Ratto, ratto, il birbone è fuggito
e ad un tratto di vista m'uscì.

ANTONIO:
He landed, and the criminal ran
away beyond the point that I
could see him.

SUSANNA:
[piano a Figaro]
Sai che il paggio . . .

FIGARO:
[piano a Susanna]
So tutto, lo vidi.
[forte, ridendo]
Ah, ah, ah, ah!

IL CONTE:
Taci là.

ANTONIO:
[a Figaro]
Cosa ridi?

FIGARO:
[ad Antonio]
Tu sei cotto dal sorger del dì.

IL CONTE:
[ad Antonio]
Or ripetimi: un uom dal balcone—

ANTONIO:
Dal balcone . . .

IL CONTE:
In giardino . . .

ANTONIO:
In giardino . . .

SUSANNA:
[softly to Figaro]
You know that the page . . .

FIGARO:
[quietly to Susanna]
I know it all, I saw him.
[loud, laughing]
Ha, ha, ha, ha!

COUNT:
Be quiet there.

ANTONIO:
[to Figaro]
What's so funny?

FIGARO:
[to Antonio]
You're drunk from daybreak
onwards.

COUNT:
[to Antonio]
Now tell me again: a man from
the balcony—

ANTONIO:
From the balcony . . .

COUNT:
In the garden . . .

ANTONIO:
In the garden . . .

SUSANNA, LA CONTESSA
& FIGARO:
Ma, signore,
se in lui parla il vino!

SUSANNA, COUNTESS
& FIGARO:
But, my lord,
it's the wine speaking!

IL CONTE:
[ad Antonio]
Segui pure, né in volto il vedesti?

COUNT:
[to Antonio]
Continue anyway, did you see his
face?

ANTONIO:
No, nol vidi.

ANTONIO:
No, I didn't.

SUSANNA & LA CONTESSA:
[piano a Figaro]
Olá, Figaro, ascolta!

SUSANNA & COUNTESS:
[quietly to Figaro]
Hey, Figaro, listen!

FIGARO:
[ad Antonio]
Via, piangione, sta zitto una volta,

per tre soldi far tanto tumulto!
Giacché il fatto non può star occulto,
sono io stesso saltato di lì.

FIGARO:
[to Antonio]
Go, you old crank, do shut up for
one minute!
To make such a fuss over nothing!
Since the truth can't be hidden
any longer, I myself jumped from
there.

IL CONTE:
Chi? Voi stesso?

COUNT:
Who? You?

SUSANNA & LA CONTESSA:
Che testa! Che ingegno!

SUSANNA & COUNTESS:
What a brain! What genius!

FIGARO:
[al Conte]
Che stupor!

FIGARO:
[to the Count]
What confusion!

ANTONIO:
[a Figaro]
Chi? Voi stesso?

IL CONTE:
Già creder nol posso.

ANTONIO:
[a Figaro]
Come mai diventaste sì grosso?
Dopo il salto non foste così.

FIGARO:
A chi salta succede così.

ANTONIO:
Chi'l direbbe?

SUSANNA & LA CONTESSA:
[a Figaro]
Ed insiste quel pazzo!

IL CONTE:
[ad Antonio]
Tu che dici?

ANTONIO:
A me parve il ragazzo.

IL CONTE:
Cherubin!

SUSANNA & LA CONTESSA:
Maledetto!

FIGARO:
Esso appunto

ANTONIO:
[to Figaro]
Who? It was you?

COUNT:
I just don't believe it.

ANTONIO:
[to Figaro]
How did you grow so big?
You didn't look that size when
you jumped.

FIGARO:
It happens to people when they
jump.

ANTONIO:
Who says that?

SUSANNA & COUNTESS:
[to Figaro]
The fool persists!

COUNT:
[to Antonio]
What do you say?

ANTONIO:
It looked to me like the boy.

COUNT:
Cherubino!

SUSANNA & COUNTESS:
Damn!

FIGARO:
So of course

da Siviglia a cavallo qui giunto,	he rode all the way back here from Seville by horse,
da Siviglia ov'ei forse sarà.	When by now he must already be in Seville.

ANTONIO:	ANTONIO:
Questo no, questo no,	No, not that way.
che il cavallo	I didn't see a horse
io non vidi saltare di là.	jump from there.

IL CONTE:	COUNT:
Che pazienza! Finiam questo ballo!	I'm out of patience! Let's finish this silliness!

SUSANNA & LA CONTESSA:	SUSANNA & COUNTESS:
Come mai, giusto ciel, finirà?	Good heavens, how will this end?

IL CONTE:	COUNT:
[a Figaro]	[to Figaro]
Dunque tu . . .	So you . . .

FIGARO:	FIGARO:
Saltai giù.	I jumped down.

IL CONTE:	COUNT:
Ma perché?	But why?

FIGARO:	FIGARO:
Il timor . . .	Fear . . .

IL CONTE:	COUNT:
Che timor?	Fear of what?

FIGARO:	FIGARO:
[additando la camera delle serve]	[indicating the servant's quarters]
Là rinchiuso	Locked in there, waiting
aspettando quel caro visetto . . .	for a glimpse of that dear face . . .
Tippe tappe, un sussurro fuor d'uso,	Tap, tap, I heard a strange sound . . .

voi gridaste! lo scritto biglietto,

saltai giù dal terrore confuso . . .

[fingendo d'aversi stroppiato
il piede]

you shouted! I thought about the
letter . . .

I jumped down in panic,
confused . . .

[fakes a limp]

Wonderful harmony here as the retard gives the impression of exaggerated suffering. The tempo changes to andante (moderate walking tempo), which seems to be the speed at which the Count conducts his interrogations. Note how marvelously Mozart manages this transition, with his musical evocation of Figaro's limp offering the perfect excuse to slow things down in preparation for the big climax to come. Clarinets also return to the wind section.

e stravolto m'ho un nervo del piè!

ANTONIO:
[porgendo a Figaro alcune
carte chiuse]
Vostre dunque saran queste carte
che perdeste . . .

IL CONTE:
[togliendogliele]
Olà, porgile a me.

FIGARO:
[piano alla Contessa e Susanna]

Sono in trappola.

SUSANNA & LA CONTESSA:
[piano a Figaro]
Figaro, all'erta.

IL CONTE:
[apre il foglio e lo chiude tosto]

Dite un po', questo foglio cos'è?

and I pulled a muscle in my foot!

ANTONIO:
[making to give Figaro
some folded papers]
Then these must be the papers
you lost . . .

COUNT:
[taking them from him]
Here, give them to me.

FIGARO:
[quietly to the Countess and
Susanna]
Now I'm trapped.

SUSANNA & COUNTESS:
[quietly to Figaro]
Figaro, watch out!

COUNT:
[opens the papers and then closes
them]
Tell me now, what are these?

FIGARO:
[cavando di tasca alcune
carte per guardare]
Tosto, tosto . . .
ne ho tanti—aspettate.

ANTONIO:
Sarà forse il sommario de' debiti.

FIGARO:
No, la lista degl'osti.

IL CONTE:
[a Figaro]
Parlate.
[ad Antonio]
E tu lascialo; e parti.

SUSANNA, LA CONTESSA
& FIGARO:
[ad Antonio]
Lascialo/Lasciami, e parti.

ANTONIO:
Parto, sì, ma se torno a trovarti—

FIGARO:
Vanne, vanne, non temo di te.

[parte Antonio]

FIGARO:
[taking some other papers out of
his pockets to look at them]
Just a minute . . .
I have so many—wait a bit.

ANTONIO:
Perhaps it's a summary of your
debts.

FIGARO:
No, it's the list of taverns and
bars.

COUNT:
[to Figaro]
Speak.
[to Antonio]
And you let him alone; and leave.

SUSANNA, COUNTESS
& FIGARO:
[to Antonio]
Let him/me alone, and leave.

ANTONIO:
I'm going, yes, but if I return and
find you—

FIGARO:
Go, go, I'm not afraid of you.

[Antonio leaves]

The interrogation continues, in a more sinister minor key.

IL CONTE:
[riapre la carta e poi tosto
la chiude; a Figaro]
Dunque . . .

COUNT:
[glances over the papers
again; to Figaro]
Well, then . . .

LA CONTESSA:
[piano a Susanna]
O ciel! La patente del paggio!

SUSANNA:
[piano a Figaro]
Giusti Dei, la patente!

IL CONTE:
[a Figaro]
Coraggio!

FIGARO:
Uh, che testa! Questa è la patente
che poc'anzi il fanciullo mi die'.

IL CONTE:
Per che fare?

FIGARO:
Vi manca . . .

IL CONTE:
Vi manca?

LA CONTESSA:
[piano a Susanna]
Il suggello.

SUSANNA:
[piano a Figaro]
Il suggello.

IL CONTE:
Rispondi.

FIGARO:
È l'usanza . . .

COUNTESS:
[quietly to Susanna]
Oh heavens! The page's
commission!

SUSANNA:
[quietly to Figaro]
Merciful Gods, the commission!

COUNT:
[to Figaro]
Let's hear it!

FIGARO:
Oh, of course! It's the commission
the boy gave to me a short while
ago.

COUNT:
Why did he do that?

FIGARO:
It was missing . . .

COUNT:
It was missing?

COUNTESS:
[quietly to Susanna]
The seal.

SUSANNA:
[quietly to Figaro]
The seal.

COUNT:
Answer.

FIGARO:
It's usual . . .

IL CONTE:

Su via, ti confondi?

COUNT:

Are you done? Do you quit?

A short crescendo to a brief moment of triumph:

FIGARO:

È l'usanza di porvi il suggello.

FIGARO:

It's usual to provide a seal.

IL CONTE:

[guarda e vede che manca il
sigillo; guasta il foglio
e con somma collera lo getta]
(Questo birbo mi toglie il cervello,
tutto, tutto è un mistero per me.)

COUNT:

[looks and sees that it's missing
a seal; tears the paper very angrily
and drops it on the ground]
(This character has got me,
everything's still a mystery to me.)

SUSANNA & LA CONTESSA:

(Se mi salvo da questa tempesta
più non avvi naufragio per me.)

SUSANNA & COUNTESS:

(If I survive this storm
I won't have to deal with a ship-
wreck.)

FIGARO:

(Sbuffa invano e la terra calpesta;

poverino ne sa men di me.)

FIGARO:

(He pants and scuffs at the
ground in vain;
the poor little guy knows even
less than I do.)

*Tempo: allegro assai (very fast), with the full orchestra, including trumpets and
timpani. As the following exchanges proceed, you will notice that for the purpose
of making a grand musical climax, Mozart treats his seven singers as two choruses,
with Figaro, Susanna, and the Countess making up one vocal unit and everyone
else comprising the other.*

MARCELLINA, BASILIO
& BARTOLO:

[al Conte]

Voi signor, che giusto siete
ci dovete ascoltar.

MARCELLINA, BASILIO
& BARTOLO:

[to the Count]

You, my lord, who are so just,
must hear what we have to say.

IL CONTE:
(Son venuti a vendicarmi
io mi sento a consolar.)

SUSANNA, LA CONTESSA
& FIGARO:
(Son venuti a sconcertarmi
qual rimedio ritrovar?)

FIGARO:
[al Conte]
Son tre stolidi, tre pazzi,
cosa mai vengono a far?

IL CONTE:
Pian pianin, senza schiamazzi
dica ognun quel che gli par.

MARCELLINA:
Un impegno nuziale
ha costui con me contratto.
E pretendo che il contratto
deva meco effettuar.

SUSANNA, LA CONTESSA
& FIGARO:
Come! Come!

IL CONTE:
Olà, silenzio!
Io son qui per giudicar.

BARTOLO:
Io da lei scelto avvocato
vengo a far le sue difese,
le legittime pretese,
io qui vengo a palesar.

COUNT:
(They have come to avenge me
I'm feeling better already.)

SUSANNA, COUNTESS
& FIGARO:
(They've come to harm me; what
can we do to fix the situation?)

FIGARO:
[to the Count]
They're three nuts, three fools,
what could they possibly have
come for?

COUNT:
Quiet, quiet, without interrup-
tions let everyone have their say.

MARCELLINA:
This man has entered into
an agreement to marry me.
And I intend that the contract
be fulfilled.

SUSANNA, COUNTESS
& FIGARO:
What! What!

COUNT:
Hey, silence!
I'm the one who will judge.

BARTOLO:
I, as her lawyer,
come here in her defense,
in order to uphold
her legitimate claim.

SUSANNA, LA CONTESSA
& FIGARO:
È un birbante!

SUSANNA, COUNTESS
& FIGARO:
He's a scoundrel!

IL CONTE:
Olà, silenzio!
Io son qui per giudicar.

COUNT:
Hey, silence!
I am the one who will judge.

BASILIO:
Io, com'uom al mondo cognito
vengo qui per testimonio
del promesso matrimonio
con prestanza di danar.

BASILIO:
I, known as a man of good reputation, come here to testify
to the promise of marriage
in exchange for a loan of money.

SUSANNA, LA CONTESSA
& FIGARO:
Son tre matti.

SUSANNA, COUNTESS
& FIGARO:
They're three lunatics.

IL CONTE:
Olà, silenzio! Lo vedremo,
il contratto leggeremo,
tutto in ordin deve andar.

COUNT:
Silence! We'll have a look and
review the contract,
everything must be in order.

Tempo: più allegro (more quickly), then prestissimo (as fast as possible)—the big windup. Don't worry about catching the words. From this point on, purely musical considerations take over and sheer sonic splendor is everything. Even so, Mozart preserves the basic characters of the participants through the simple fact that the Susanna, Countess, and Figaro group contains the two highest voices and so they naturally dominate the ensemble with their more elaborate and long-breathed lines, while the "bad guys" mutter in gossipy fashion beneath.

SUSANNA, LA CONTESSA
& FIGARO:
Son confusa/o, son stordita/o,
disperata/o, sbalordita/o.
Certo un diavol dell'inferno
qui li ha fatti capitar.

SUSANNA, COUNTESS
& FIGARO:
I'm confused, I'm appalled,
desperate, shocked.
Certainly a devil from hell
sent them here.

MARCELLINA, BASILIO, BARTOLO & IL CONTE:	MARCELLINA, BASILIO, BARTOLO & COUNT:
Che bel colpo, che bel caso!	What good luck, what happy circumstance!
È cresciuto a tutti il naso,	It's all heading towards the end,
qualche nume a noi propizio	what god suggested
qui ci/li ha fatti capitar.	that we/they should come here?

As you can clearly see (and hear), this finale not only offers a steadily increasing range of brilliance and excitement, through changes in both tempo and orchestration, but it begins as a duet and grows naturally into a trio, a quartet, a quintet, and finally a septet. The effect is of one giant crescendo from beginning to end, and although the music falls into clear sections, it's also unquestionably a single, organic whole. I wouldn't be at all surprised if after following the entire thing, you find yourself amazed that the time has passed so quickly. It's music that really does cheat the clock.

The other point worth highlighting is similar to the one made regarding the opening scene of *Così fan tutte,* which is that by the time plot and action cease and pure ensemble music takes over at the very end, it has been so well prepared by what has come before, and the transitions so effortlessly effected, that the increased musical excitement flows directly from the operation of the story itself and comes as the inevitable release of accumulated dramatic tension. Mozart's action music, then, aside from allowing for the natural progress of events (and reaction to them) in real time, always leads by degrees to a brilliant musical apotheosis that never sounds like an artificial appendage tacked onto the end of an act or scene well after the important action has stopped.

The following discussion of Mozart's seven greatest operas will generally take his mastery of the musico-dramatic momentum just described for granted, if only because there's no way to discuss it further other than to play complete operas (or large chunks of them), and this is really an activity perfect for home listening. Not all of these works are equally successful in this regard, nor, given the varied circumstances of their creation and the subgenres to which they belong, do all of them strive to be. Now that you know what to listen for, you can very easily judge this quality for yourself by enjoying at leisure each work in turn, as time permits.

In considering the operas individually, then, I will focus principally on the way Mozart creates emotionally complete, complex characters that excite the audience's sympathy and understanding no matter how curious or contrived the situations in which they sometimes find themselves. He does this through his use of the orchestra, his style of vocal writing, his attention to the relationship between text and music, and the amount of time he allots to each character—both in solo arias and ensembles. Despite what might appear on the surface to be an opera's formidable length and complexity, Mozart's greatest gift was his ability (as heard in considering "Porgi amor") to sketch out a character with extraordinary completeness in a very short amount of time. Exploring the way he does this in the major operas reveals an endlessly fascinating and rich array of personalities cloaked in unfailingly accurate, always beautiful, and directly expressive musical garb.

Idomeneo
1780

Introduction

*I*domeneo is Mozart's ninth opera, and the first that practically everyone agrees belongs with the great works. Beyond that opinions vary widely, from "incomparably the greatest opera seria ever written" to "wonderful in parts but on the whole dull." The first judgment strikes me as ridiculous on its face (remember Handel?), the second as too simplistic. On the other hand, it's not unusual to hear those familiar with the opera express the opinion that it would have been nice if Mozart simply had let Neptune's voracious sea monster devour Crete and all of its inhabitants at the end of act 2, making for a powerfully tragic conclusion and saving the audience from having to deal with act 3. Even then the work would still last about two and half hours, and indeed its partisans sometimes see the opera as offering "too much of a good thing."

This may sound like damning with faint praise, but the fact is that nothing in the above paragraph would raise much objection from Mozart, who was well aware that his music was great but that the opera as a whole was problematic. His letters home during rehearsals stress the need to shorten, tighten, and make the action more natural. There's absolutely no question that Mozart did everything he could under the circumstances to create as much purely musical continuity as possible, but that wasn't really the problem. In fact, one of the reasons the opera is less well known than it should be may stem from the fact that so many of the best arias remain open-ended, running directly into a new recitative or chorus, and so they require some tinkering prior to independent performance in recital programs.

Some commentators blame the outmoded conventions of opera seria, with its slow-moving sequence of arias and recitatives, for the drama's tendency to drag, despite Mozart's best efforts. However, criticizing the genre itself isn't a terribly useful point of view today, when opera seria has made an unprecedented comeback (especially the theoretically even more fusty baroque kind), often playing to full houses the world over. A good opera seria does indeed maintain a powerful feeling of dramatic pacing (Mozart's own *La clemenza di Tito* proves it), even if it's not achieved in the same way or at the same speed as in other kinds of opera.

The truth is that you can't evaluate theatrical viability based on a priori assumptions about musical forms and genres gleaned from a glance at a score. You have to spend the time and money in putting together the best possible production of the work in question and then see what happens in performance on stage. Despite the well-worn mythological plot and its adherence to certain time-honored conventions, there's really little musical precedent for what Mozart produced in *Idomeneo*. The work represents a revolution in the history of opera—perhaps the most advanced piece, relatively speaking, in Mozart's entire output. Like most revolutions, the process was not neat and tidy, nor was it uniformly successful. What Mozart achieved in *Idomeneo* was an unusually tight fusion of words and music, principally by enriching the sophistication, complexity, and importance of the orchestra to an unheard of degree, but always with the object of better articulating the feelings and emotions of the characters.

#	Title	Flutes	Oboes	Clarinets	Bassoons	Horns	Trumpets	Timpani
	Idomeneo: Quick Reference							
	Orchestration (in Addition to Strings)							
	Act 1							
1	Aria: Padre, germani, addio!		2		2	2		
2	Aria: Non ho colpa		2	2	2	2		
3	Chorus: Godiam la pace		2		2	2		
4	Aria: Tutte nel cor	2	2		2	4		
5	Chorus: Pietà! Numi	2	2		2	4		
6	Aria: Vedrommi intorno	2	2	2	2	2		
7	Aria: Il padre adorato	1	1		1	2		
8	March	2	2		2	2	2	yes
9	Chorus: Nettuno s'onori!	2	2		2	2	2	yes
	Act 2							
10	Aria: Se il tuo duol		2			2		
11	Aria: Se il padre perdei	1	1		1	1		
12	Aria: Fuor del mar	2	2		2	2	2	yes
13	Aria: Idol mio			strings only				
14	March	2	2	2	2	2	2	yes
15	Chorus: Placido è il mar	2		2		2		
16	Trio: Pria di partir, O Dio!		2			2		
17	Chorus: Qual nuovo terrore!	2 + piccolo	2		2	4		
18	Chorus: Corriamo	2	2		2	4	2	yes
	Act 3							
19	Aria: Zeffiretti lusinghieri	2		2	2	2		
20	Duet: S'io non moro		2		2	2		
21	Quartet: Andrò ramingo e solo	2		2	2	2		
22	Aria: Se colò ne' fati			strings only				
23	Recitative: Volgi intorno	2	2		2	4	2	yes
24	Chorus: O voto tremendo	2	2		2	2	2	yes
25	March		2					
26	Aria w/Chorus: Accogli, o rè	2	2	2	2	2		
27	Aria: No, la morte		2			2		
28	Recitative: Ha vinto amore	2	2		2	2	2 (+3 trombones)	yes
29	Aria: D'Oreste, d'Ajace	2	2		2	4	2	yes
30	Recitative: Popoli! A voi			2		2		
31	Aria: Torna la pace			2	2	2		
32	Chorus: Scenda Amor	2	2		2	2	2	yes

Table of Individual Numbers and Orchestration

Idomeneo's closest aesthetic equivalent, then, is undoubtedly French grand opera of the nineteenth century, of the sort composed and made famous by Meyerbeer. Rossini's *William Tell* also offers a useful point of comparison. One finds in *Idomeneo* the same combination of public ceremony and private passion characteristic of that intentionally monumental artifact of high romanticism. As in grand opera, thrilling choruses alternate with intimate scenes of affection between man and woman, or father and son. But the opera is not primarily a romance. It details the complex interactions between conflicting emotions of love (both the Platonic and erotic varieties), honor, duty, and vengeance.

Arguably the most important single character is not any one person but rather "the people" in the form of the chorus, and the relationship between the monarch and his subjects is as important as any of the more intimate subplots. It is these larger-than-life issues (and characters) that separate opera seria from opera buffa. Serious opera need not end tragically (*Idomeneo* doesn't), just as comic opera is funny not because it is silly or full of jokes but because it is about romantic love, and when it comes to this kind of relationship, most people behave like fools at some point and get themselves into ridiculous situations. As Mozart so brilliantly realized, a comedy about people who take themselves and their situations completely seriously allows for the possibility of the growth and development of individual personalities over the course of the drama, and this, rather than the obligatory and usually rather mechanical plot resolution at the end, becomes the real subject of the opera.

By definition this sort of realism cannot exist in opera seria, where the actors are invariably noble, heroic, and good, or quite irredeemably evil; where the nature of the relationships involves more than just the barriers to a marriage; and where one (or more) of the principals isn't an individual but a collective entity—whether a society, a city, or even an entire country.

The various characters cannot change substantially as the opera progresses, nor would audiences want them to. Nothing would be more dramatically frustrating than to have a composer build up a heroic portrait, aria after aria, of a major role, only to have the audience discover at the last minute that the hero is really a coward. The problem in working with music is that everything takes time; in general, the more intense and serious the emotion being expressed, the more reinforcement it requires and the more time it necessarily takes to make a positive impression.

It's easy to understand, then, that when the subject of the opera moves away from the familiar feelings of normal people to take on big issues, such as the conflict between love and duty or good and evil, there's not much room for the kind of ambivalence that allows a composer to paint his portraits in subtle shades. Specific emotions must be distributed among the characters, rather than concentrated within them in ever-shifting proportions. Accordingly, each aria represents a frozen moment in time expressing a single emotional state with as much force as possible, a musical snapshot of a character whose basic qualities are fixed more or less from the very beginning. Within this constraint, you will surely agree that Mozart's unparalleled gift for expressing emotion operates as powerfully in *Idomeneo* as in any later work, because what moves listeners is the fact that the feelings themselves are truly and accurately communicated through the music.

Idomeneo was commissioned to open the 1780–81 carnival season in Munich, the city with the finest opera house in Europe at the time. The prestige was enormous, particularly for Mozart, who was anxious to get out of Salzburg and make a career for himself in the world at large. As was typical in works written to special commission, he was not given his choice of subject. His librettist, Giambattista Varesco, was concerned that every word of his already-too-lengthy poem be set faithfully. Mozart, with uncharacteristic diplomacy, got him to make some worthwhile changes for the sake of the action, and he also knew perfectly well that he would have to make adjustments and tailor the music to the specific abilities (or lack thereof) of the singers once the work went into rehearsal. Then he simply pulled out all the stops in a determined effort to create the grandest of grand operas, leaving a trail of revisions, second thoughts, and optional alternatives in his wake that only make modern choices between them even more complicated.

A complete performance of *Idomeneo,* which Mozart never saw or even expected, would run about three and a half hours (including its ballet sequence). Absolute length isn't really the issue, though: Wagner's operas routinely run longer. What matters most is dramatic continuity, the ability of the composer to build excitement as each act proceeds. You will not find that quality strongly in evidence here. There is nothing comparable to, for example, the fluid action in the act 2 finale to *The Marriage of Figaro,* discussed in "Mozart's Operatic Style" (and available on CD track 8). Instead Mozart presents some impressive choruses and some very rare (for him) nature painting: music evocative of storms and the sea. It's monumental and extremely effective, indeed unique in his mature output, but still essentially static, a sequence of bold tableaux.

And yet, the opera contains great music. If you look at the table of individual numbers and their scoring, you will find Mozart seizing the opportunity to use the largest possible orchestra of his time with an especially lavish hand. There's a piccolo screaming above the chorus that describes the arrival of the sea monster, the agent of the god Neptune's anger. Trombones provide the same god's voice at the opera's end in a tiny accompanied recitative lasting only a few bars (that Mozart revised at least three times). You will meet these instruments again, on a much more elaborate scale, in *Don Giovanni* and *The Magic Flute.*

Uniquely in his mature operas, Mozart has four horns instead of the usual two, and in the act 2 march (No. 14), he asks that the brass and timpani use mutes, a most unusual effect for its time. Most important, this is the opera in which Mozart pioneered the various uses of the clarinet, the instrument that more than any other became his personal musical calling card—particularly in music evocative of yearning, a melancholy desire for love or simple human warmth.

It may be that were it never known what Mozart achieved later in his life, *Idomeneo* would be judged differently. Hindsight can be cruel to art. The opera has in fact achieved a good measure of success on records, where listeners can take as much or as little of the music as they please, confident that just about all of it is good and the only significant issue is how much time they have to invest.

In live performance, though, the cost and difficulty of a stage production and the necessity to prune the piece back to a manageable length often wind up serving neither the work nor the public especially well. Moreover, one should not take Mozart to task for demonstrating everything that he was capable of doing in a single score of epic length: how could he know if he would ever have another chance? So rather than harping on what he would very shortly learn to do even better in future operas, the remainder of this discussion will instead focus on the many things that he already does supremely well right here—so well, in fact, that no other composer of the time could touch him.

Music and Characters

In the following discussion, I will use the characters' Italian names as found in the libretto, as opposed to the English equivalents (for example, Idomeneo rather than Idomeneus). If you come across other writings on the opera in books, theatrical programs, or recording notes, you may see them either way, and indeed I use the English versions in discussing *La clemenza di Tito*. Neither is inherently preferable and there are no hard and fast rules, so I offer the chance to see it done both ways. This issue generally arises only in connection with Latin or mythological characters that have familiar identities in English literature as well.

In his later operas, Mozart gives most of his principal roles two full solo arias each (or one per act). As you can see from the list below, here they each have three, with the exception of Arbace, Idomeneo's earnest but dull confidant, whose role is the least important and therefore the first to go in most stage productions (and one that need not be considered any further). Most of these arias are magnificent, if somewhat long on average, and show Mozart at his very best.

Character	Arias
Idomeneo	3 + 1 with chorus (No. 26)
Ilia	3
Idamante	3
Elettra	3
Arbace	2

Curiously, the number of solo ensembles is not large: one duet, one trio, and one (very fine) quartet, and this only serves to further emphasize the fact that the interaction between the characters does not take place in the kind of action music that Mozart later mastered to such dazzling effect, but rather in the recitatives. On the other hand, there are no fewer than nine choruses, making "the people" very much a participant in the drama, deserving the same consideration as any of the major characters.

Overture

The first of Mozart's great opera overtures, this one does not quote any of the themes to come, but does provide an excellent summary of the moods of the drama, being alternately stormy, brooding, heroic, and lyrical. It is an introduction in the truest sense, both anticipating what will occur and acting as an effective contrast to the gentleness of Ilia's opening scene. Indeed, the only thing that keeps this overture out of the orchestral repertoire is the fact that it ends quietly, via a very impressively executed diminuendo and gradual draining of tension, so as to make an effective transition to Ilia's ensuing accompanied recitative. Otherwise the music is certainly as fine as anything that Mozart achieved later.

Idomeneo

When the opera opens, Idomeneo, the king of Crete, has been away at the Trojan Wars for twenty years. On his return, his fleet encountered a terrible storm at sea, and in order to appease the god Neptune, he has promised to sacrifice the first person he sees on reaching shore. Naturally this turns out to be Idamante, his own son, and so for the next three and a half hours, Idomeneo finds himself torn between love for his child and a desire to save him, and his duty, for the sake of his people, to fulfill his oath. When first encountered, he has just landed on shore and is already having second thoughts about the bargain he struck with Neptune.

His first aria, "Vedrommi intorno" (No. 6), with its rich scoring for full wind section, expresses his gratitude at reaching land, but the tempo quickens as remorse immediately assails him and his thoughts turn to the victim who must pay in blood for his safe arrival. As with so many of the arias in this opera, the music segues directly into the following secco (simple) rec-itative. Idomeneo's act 2 aria, "Fuor del mar" (No. 12), is the opera's showstopper. Brutally difficult and very long (more than six minutes), the scoring for trumpets and drums reinforces the heroic cast of the king's character, while the hellishly intricate vocal coloratura perfectly underlines the turmoil he feels at send-ing his son away from Crete, preserving his life but breaking his oath to the god. This is really powerful, vintage opera seria stuff, in which vocal display heightens the intensity of the emotions being expressed. Here, Mozart treats his audience to an emphatic ending that positively invites applause.

The aria with chorus, "Acogli, o rè" (No. 26), is basically a set piece, an invocation preceding the sacrifice of Idamante in the temple of Neptune. It reveals nothing new about Idomeneo but presents him in his public capacity as leader of his people, a nec-essary contrast to the personal expression contained in the solo arias. And speaking of personal, "Torna la pace" (No. 31) is not only the most purely beautiful piece in the entire opera, it rep-resents a milestone in the history of Mozart's art. As Idomeneo sings "Peace returns to my heart; my spent love returns, and I feel young," pairs of clarinets and bassoons warble contentedly over and under the vocal line.

Here, and in Ilia's aria "Zeffiretti lusinghieri" (No. 19), we encounter two of the earliest examples of the orchestral color-ation that Mozart almost invariably turns to whenever he wants to express the emotions of love, gentle melancholy, and sadness. For Idomeneo's rebirth is also an ending of sorts: he abdicates his role as king in favor of Idamante and becomes an ordinary citizen, and Mozart's setting also achieves the remarkable goal of turning the hero into an ordinary human being. The proud but troubled king we met at the beginning of the opera ends it as a loving father.

Strictly speaking, this about-face violates the conventions of opera seria, and in the original version of the story that Veresco worked from, the piece ends tragically, with the sacrifice of Idamante. It is precisely this revision, however, than allows Mozart the single opportunity in the entire work to reveal the sort of growth of character that becomes the watchword of his style in the Italian comedies, and so eagerly does he seize the chance that the incongruity of Idamante's sudden reprieve becomes a dead issue as soon as Idomeneo begins singing.

There's one more interesting fact about Idomeneo. He is not a castrato (Idamante has that distinction), but a tenor. This is a reflection of local conditions, for the lead singer in Munich was a famous (if aging) tenor. Unlike in later romantic opera, the heroic tenor lead was not common in Mozart's day. In the Italian comedies, the lead singers tend to be baritones (Figaro and Don Giovanni, for example), and Mozart treats the high male voice just as he does the high female voice, requiring extraordinary flexibility and agility. Already in 1786, when Mozart arranged a private performance of *Idomeneo,* he shortened and simplified "Fuor del mar." If one factors in "Torna la pace" as well, no other tenor role in his mature operas, difficult as some of them are, comes close to this one in terms of its extravagant demands on the voice.

The simple truth is that until the recent rebirth of opera seria and the consequent training of singers technically able to meet it on its own terms, there were few tenors around who could handle Idomeneo's music. Certainly a singer trained in the nineteenth-century tradition of Verdi and Wagner, where power is everything, would never dare to take on the lead in this opera. In Mozart's day, opera houses were not so large, and a finished technique was much more highly prized than sheer volume and amplitude. So it's all well and good to examine the causes for an opera's neglect in purely musical terms, but the fact remains that even the gravest aesthetic reservations must ultimately yield to practical matters, and if no one can sing the bloody thing in the first place, then all other issues effectively become moot.

Ilia

Ilia is a Trojan princess, daughter of King Priam (now deceased), held in captivity along with a varied assortment of her compatriots. She is a familiar character in opera: the sweet lyric soprano who spends most of her time feeling sad, be it for her lost homeland or the love she feels for Idamante and the guilt that this engenders. He, after all, is the son of the enemy king. So she too finds herself torn between love and duty, although by the standards of Idomeneo, her dilemma is less dire. That said, the music Mozart gives her is anything but conventional. In a word, it's gorgeous. She is first cousin to the Countess in *Figaro* and Pamina in *The Magic Flute*. In her first aria, "Padre, germani" (No. 1), she bids farewell to her fellow Trojans (symbolically), expressing sadness at her situation through the melancholy vocal line and the reedy tone of the oboe, the archetypical instrument for musical expressions of lamentation.

Ilia's second aria, "Se il padre" (No. 11), is a touchstone for the way in which Mozart uses instrumental color to enrich the vocal line and intensify emotional expression. Less a solo aria than a sort of quintet for flute, oboe, bassoon, horn, and voice (with string accompaniment), the sense of the music is the exact opposite of what was heard in Ilia's first aria. Now, she says, Crete is her home, and she will happily forget her anguished past and look forward to a new life. At times it's hard to tell if the singer imitates the solo winds or if the winds follow her: they operate on a plane of absolute equality, and from a technical point of view, this aria represents the epitome of Mozartean bel canto, requiring perfect intonation, seamless legato phrasing, and a real trill—nothing breaks the magical mood more thoroughly than a botched vocal imitation of an instrumental gesture when the entire point of the music is the creation of a euphonious chorus of lyrical melody.

This aria is also remarkable from another perspective, as it runs directly into the following accompanied recitative of Idomeneo. So unusual is Ilia's happiness that the king immediately guesses the underlying cause: she and Idamante are in love. As Idomeneo ponders Ilia's feelings, Mozart quotes bits of her aria, gradually introducing new music as the implications of this new revelation sink in, until the recitative flows without pause into the next number, "Fuor del mar." The musical continuity is as absolute as in any later, more theoretically advanced sort of writing, and the contrast between the two arias—one introverted, the other extraverted—is extremely effective.

Ilia's final aria, "Zeffiretti lusinghieri" (No. 19), expresses the longing of a woman in love. As previously mentioned, it's one of the two arias in the opera in which Mozart employs the instrumental combination that would come to characterize almost all of his future love music: pairs of clarinets, bassoons, and horns, with optional flutes. The effect here, as elsewhere, is exquisite. Like her previous aria, this one leads directly into the following recitative. Aside from these three lovely, gentle solos, Ilia has an important part in the act 3 duet with Idamante, "S'io non moro" (No. 20), and in the big quartet that follows, which is far and away the most important ensemble piece in the entire opera.

This means that she remains onstage singing through the first three numbers of the third act, or for nearly twenty minutes of music including recitatives, a tall order by any standard. The attention Mozart gives her justifies itself, however, in the climactic temple scene just before the end, where Ilia's offer to sacrifice herself to save Idamante's life compels the god Neptune to spare him. Although brief, this bit of accompanied recitative is quite moving and gives the character a welcome bit of back-bone. One might say that Ilia resolves the conflict between love and duty not in favor of one or the other, but by realizing that love *is* her duty.

Idamante

Compared to Ilia or Idomeneo, Idamante comes as a shock. The role was originally written for a not-very-good castrato (which doesn't mean that the music is bad) and later revised for a tenor. This solution isn't entirely satisfactory, because both Idomeneo and Arbace are also tenors (all the more reason to dump Arbace if you have a tenor Idamante), and while both Ilia and Elettra are sopranos, their music and vocal timbres are quite different (Ilia is a light lyric; Elettra requires a much heavier and more powerful voice). In most performances today, then, Idamante's part goes to a mezzo-soprano or contralto. He is, to put it bluntly, a drip. His love is pure, his sense of duty dominant, he suffers nobly, kills the sea monster (offstage, alas), then selflessly agrees to die to let his dad and country off the hook. By the end of the opera, you kind of wish that Varesco hadn't changed the ending of the original French tragedy on which his libretto is based and spared Idamante's life.

Characters such as this leave a composer few options other than to write attractive, earnest music, and Mozart does what he can. In his first aria, "Non ho colpa" (No. 2), Idamante asks Ilia (for more than six minutes) not to hold him responsible for her suffering but to acknowledge his love for her. When she refuses, it's all one can do not to shout "You go, girl!" In his second aria, "Il padre adorato" (No. 7), Idamante expresses his grief—happily, for less than three minutes this time—at having been rebuffed by his father on their first encounter (he is unaware of Idomeneo's vow). It's a credit to Mozart in both of these numbers that he never permits his character to whine. The music has remarkable purity and directness, but to follow Ilia's first aria with Idamante's gets the opera off to a slow start (despite Idamante's aria's quicker tempo and rich scoring), dramatically speaking.

Mozart put Idamante's first two arias in act 1. His last solo, "No, la morte" (No. 27), comes at the very end of the opera, and turns out to be almost worth the wait. It's a heroic, very formal number in old-fashioned *da capo* (that is, ABA) form. Quick outer sections enclose a slow middle full of pathos, with the repeat of the A section enlivened by additional detail that subtly enhances the force of the music. Austere scoring, for pairs of oboes and horns with strings, pays obvious homage to the great baroque tradition from which the opera comes, and conveys a similar dignity. The only problem here is the silliness of the situation. Everyone is standing around waiting to get on with the sacrifice, and Idamante sings for four and a half minutes about how happy he is to die if it will save his country and the life of his beloved. Cutting the aria is out of the question: it runs right into the recitative in which Ilia offers her life in his place, and so on to the dramatic climax of the act. But Mozart did, in fact, cut it (as far as is known) at the premiere.

It's very interesting to compare Idamante with Mozart's most famous lovesick wimp, Don Ottavio, boyfriend of Donna Anna in *Don Giovanni*. In that opera, the character's too-good-to-be-true behavior is constantly undermined, both by the context (Donna Anna keeps putting off their wedding) and by the fact that his willingness to be a doormat is so enthusiastic that one begins to suspect that he must have ulterior motives. Certainly there's no possibility for that sort of cynicism here; such thoughts belong entirely to the world of comedy, or reality. Idamante is the second most allegorical character in this very allegorical work, and the sad thing is that he doesn't even come first in this particular contest. The prize goes to:

Elettra

Elettra (a.k.a. Electra) has an independent reputation beyond this particular opera. Daughter of Agamemnon and Clytemnestra (who conspired with her lover Aegistus to murder her husband), her name has become synonymous in Greek legend with female fury for helping her brother Orestes slay the guilty pair. You might call her activities here a warmup to the more famous main event: Elettra is her name, and vengeance is her game. Actually, it's vengeance mixed with intense jealousy, and that makes the role even juicier. Like the Queen of the Night in *The Magic Flute,* Elettra gets by far the most hysterical, exciting, and (for listeners) fun music in the entire opera.

Her first aria, "Tutte nel cor" (No. 4), really gets the music moving, and Mozart's setting is a true dramatic masterstroke. Elettra is in love with Idamante and is well aware that he loves Ilia. She is furious because Ilia is not just her rival but a hated princess of Troy, the enemy nation. The words of the aria are typical—"fury burns in my breast, let my rival writhe in the flames of hell and feel the full force of my cruelty and ven-geance"—that sort of thing. It's the music that's special, a roiling mass of churning strings and winds that builds to so great a rage that it spills over the bounds of the aria and becomes the chorus of shipwrecked warriors begging the gods for mercy. The way Mozart transforms the character's inner torment into an external convulsion of nature is sheer genius.

In act 2, Elettra believes that she and Idamante are about to be sent away together by Idomeneo so as to avoid the necessary sacrifice of the prince. She is thrilled, and she expresses her hap-piness in what is undoubtedly the strangest, but one of the most telling, arias in the entire opera, "Idol mio" (No. 13). Basically she says: "I don't care if you don't love me. I prefer a good chal-lenge anyway. I'll be next to you and Ilia will be far away, so under those circumstances, you don't stand much chance of refusing me for long." Love music this is not, and in order to understand what Mozart is doing, it's necessary to look at the piece from two different perspectives.

First, compare this aria to Ilia's exquisite "Se il padre," which was just heard a couple of numbers previously. Mozart denies Elettra any accompaniment other than strings. Ilia's radiance, beauty, and sensuousness find no equivalent in Elettra's music, and by refusing to let the winds of the orchestra join her, Mozart tells the audience that her vision of happiness is an illusion. This observation becomes even more credible if one compares Elettra's first hysterical outburst to this stiff, formal, emotionally cool, almost dainty aria—a self-deluded oasis of peace in her otherwise tormented soul. Coming from this character, it makes an almost surreal impression. If this were not opera seria, one might even go so far as to call it a parody, but the context speaks for itself. On its own, it remains a slightly bland expression of contentment. Heard in its proper place, it adds a new dimension to Mozart's portrait of Elettra.

Mozart had a big problem with Elettra's final aria, "D'Oreste, d'Ajace" (No. 29), which basically restates the same ideas as her first one, only in even more vicious terms and with trumpets and drums driving home the point like the explosions of mortar fire. The vocal writing really goes wild in this number, culminating at the end in a pair of hair-raising chromatic shrieks followed by downward staccato cackles, possibly the most terrifying representation of maniacal laughter in all of music. It's an absolute show-stopper of a piece, which is exactly why Mozart cut it before the first performance. As he explained it in a letter to his father, the plot has at last turned out happily, but the final chorus of rejoicing has to be delayed while everyone stands around watching Elettra have one more hysterical fit. He had a point, of course, and leaving the aria out certainly ends the opera sooner, but not necessarily better.

Elettra is an impressive character, one of the first in a line of insane soprano roles that ask less for vocal beauty than for intensity, stage presence, and a big willingness to take risks with the health of the voice by screaming one's lungs out. Some of Elettra's operatic descendants, aside from the Queen of the Night already mentioned, include Verdi's Abigaille in *Nabucco,* Kundry in Wagner's *Parsifal,* Puccini's Turandot in the eponymous opera, and most famously, Elettra herself in the form of *Elektra,* the opera by Richard Strauss that has turned out to be far more popular than *Idomeneo.* So I suppose you might say that Elettra realized her fondest dreams in the end. While she may not have gotten Idamante, she did get top billing in her very own opera, and for most divas that would be sweet revenge indeed.

The Chorus

The chorus has an important role in *Idomeneo,* and contributes significantly to the audience's understanding of, and sympathy for, the king's plight. Here is a summary of the purpose of the various choruses with which Mozart peppers the opera. As noted, there are nine of them in total:

No. 3   The chorus of grateful Trojan prisoners thanks Idamante for granting them their freedom.

No. 5   This is the chorus of frantic sailors that takes over the music from Elettra's first aria. The vocal forces are divided in two: those who have made it to shore and, offstage, those still at sea begging for mercy.

No. 9   Preceded by the first of the three marches, this finale to act 1 represents the safe return of the Cretan warriors and the welcome that they receive from the joyful populace.

No. 15   The sea is calm, and the chorus gives thanks that the war has finally passed and peace has come to Crete.

Nos. 17   These two numbers really make up a single larger
and 18   one, separated only by an extended (and dramatically inert) accompanied recitative of Idomeneo. In No. 17, a storm kicks up and the sea monster appears. The first chorus arises out of the preceding trio, in keeping with the same effective procedure heard in act 1 following Elettra's first aria. Its orchestration includes a screaming piccolo used just as Beethoven later would in the storm movement of the Sixth Symphony. The following chorus is a long, gradual diminuendo, the words of which are primarily "Let's run away!" In true operatic fashion, they sing it for a while before they actually do it, and the soft ending comes as a surprise and just a bit of an anticlimax.

No. 24   The chorus expresses horror at the impending fulfillment of Idomeneo's vow.

No. 26   Idomeneo, the high priest, the lesser priests, and the people sing a hymn to Neptune, asking him to accept the sacrifice and restore peace to the land.

No. 32   The happy ending. You get to hear this chorus twice, separated by a mimed wind-band interlude in which Idamante is made king. The instrumental writing reminds us that Mozart's greatest piece for wind ensemble, the "Gran Partita," was composed about this same time.

You can see very clearly from this list that the chorus is not one character, but many. Still, the thrust of almost all of these numbers is the same: the people suffer from the ravages of war and ask only for freedom, peace, and prosperity. They put the personal struggles of the principal actors in the drama in broader context, but there's more to it than that. It's very easy in a plot that concerns the conflict between love and duty to minimize the importance of duty. One can, after all, see Idomeneo's relationship to his son, but his role as king and consequent duty to his people remain a more abstract concept. Mozart's choruses humanize and make tangible this aspect of Idomeneo's personality, and so give meaning to what is, after all, the central dilemma on which the entire plot turns.

Whether or not this was a good idea is another story, for the presence of so many choruses achieves Mozart's evident intent, but at the sacrifice of dramatic momentum. The finale to act 1, which is marked "Intermezzo" in the score, is particularly unmotivated since it can be taken on faith that the Cretans arrive home safely. But it's also the most highly developed and substantial chorus in the entire opera, and musically it leaves nothing to be desired. Here is yet another example of the fact that the more one looks at *Idomeneo,* the clearer it becomes that its strengths are also, in fact, its weaknesses.

Take another example: joining Elettra's first aria to the ensuing chorus of shipwrecked sailors is undoubtedly a brilliant idea. On the other hand, having Ilia's glorious "Zeffiretti lusinghieri" evaporate into dry recitative, leading in turn to a comparatively dull duet between Ilia and Idamante, serves no purpose at all. This is known because Mozart cut the duet before the first performance, understandably so. Commentators on the opera frequently remark that the care Mozart takes to make seamless transitions from one number to the next constitutes one of the opera's most forward-looking features (granted) and creates powerful dramatic continuity. This last point strikes me as an unpersuasive argument, for several reasons.

In the first place, smooth musical transitions do not automatically create dramatic momentum, which depends not so much on the way one number leads to another as on whether or not each number feels the right length in and of itself, and whether or not the internal ordering creates the impression of increasing tension as each act proceeds. After all, even if the ends of most arias dovetail neatly into the ensuing pieces, the music's overall proportions remain the same. In act 1 of *Idomeneo,* those proportions are approximately 60 percent music (defined as arias and ensembles) to 40 percent recitative (both simple and accompanied). That's a lot of time spent in what amounts to conversation, and this is one of the factors that slows the piece down, expressively speaking.

Furthermore, the highly touted continuity in question here is inconsistently present and ineffectively placed on the large scale. For example, joining Ilia's second aria to the recitative leading to Idomeneo's "Fuor del mar" makes perfect dramatic sense, as does the unity created by attaching Elettra's first aria to the ensuing chorus of sailors. But note that both of these events occur toward the beginnings of the acts in question, whereas in Mozart's later operas, he proves beyond all doubt that if musical and dramatic continuity are to mean the same thing, then both need to increase in tandem as the acts progress: this means the creation of finales such as that in act 2 of *Figaro.* Indeed, it's quite significant that in his last opera seria, *La clemenza di Tito,* the practice of linking independent pieces into longer units occurs specifically at the end of each act (and the means of generating momentum from one number to the next is entirely different).

I have already observed that the placement of Elettra's final aria does not further the cause of dramatic momentum. Neither does "Torna la pace," for that matter, which was also cut before the first performance. When a composer feels obliged to remove two or three of the finest numbers in the opera (including Idamante's last aria) from what ought to be the principal climax of a very long evening simply to get the story over with more quickly, then music and drama have not been satisfactorily equalized and integrated. There's no point in further rationalization. *Idomeneo's* greatness does not reside in its construction and organization, and the "continuity" issue really is something of a red herring. In this day and age, when audiences naturally expect continuous music throughout an entire opera, it's naïve of Mozart scholars and essayists to expect that they should care about a matter that remains essentially of historical or academic interest only.

Also of academic interest is the purely philosophical question of whether or not just because the music is great, the drama must also be great. It's understandable that someone who loves this work and knows it well really doesn't care about how long unbelievers have to sit in the theater and how bored they might get in the process. But with a composer of Mozart's reputation, revered as he is, and with a score so full of richness and original- ity as regards characterization and treatment of the orchestra, that argument would have been settled long ago if it favored the opera's partisans. The fact is that the music is great—the opera, not quite. This doesn't mean it shouldn't be imaginatively pro- duced and staged, or recorded, or enjoyed for its considerable merits. Nor is it exactly a pity that we now have an additional very good reason to listen to the next six operas and discover how Mozart solved the problems that confronted him in this, his first mature stage work. Onwards!

Die Entführung aus dem Serail (The Abduction from the Seraglio)

1782

Introduction

*T*he *Abduction from the Seraglio* is a musical comedy, or singspiel, which in practical terms means spoken dialogue intermingled with songs and ensembles, just as in a Broadway musical or operetta. In Mozart's time, however, the audience expected to have real opera singers in the title roles, not merely singing actors, and this requirement elevates the music beyond the sort of musical theater most often encountered today. Otherwise there's basically no difference at all. This is Mozart's first work for Vienna following his move there in 1781, and the one with which he introduced himself to the Viennese public. It was probably his greatest theatrical success during his lifetime, although it was in fact composed for a failing venture, Emperor Joseph II's National Singspiel, which was charged with creating a decent new repertoire in German—the "language of the people." Evidently "the people" weren't terribly impressed, but they did take to Mozart's *Abduction*.

There was nothing new about the story. Ever since the Turkish siege of Vienna a century previously, stories of virtuous European women escaping from harems had been a staple of the stage. Haydn wrote a huge full-scale Italian opera in 1775 called *L'Incontro improvviso* to virtually the same plot, and comparison between the two is striking. Haydn's work lasts more than three hours and accordingly has been relegated to the "life is too short" list of works that people know about but never listen to. Mozart, composing to what he believed to be the Viennese taste for keeping things short and perky (is taste really that different anywhere?), covers all of the same ground in a couple of hours, and even then he shortened several of the arias prior to the first performance to keep things moving smartly along.

Both works, however, share a particular orchestral brilliance on account of their use of what were called "Turkish" instruments, or "Janissary music," consisting at a minimum of bass drum, cymbals, and triangle, with optional additions of other sorts of authentic jangling percussion, such as tambourine or the so-called Turkish crescent (a long stick hung with metal bits that rattle when shaken). These were to the Turkish military what trumpets and timpani were to the European, and it's worth keeping in mind in this respect that in Mozart's day, most trumpeters did double duty in their local regiment, and timpani, when needed for concerts, would have been requisitioned from the armory and were more commonly seen on horseback than in a symphony orchestra. It was not until Haydn's "Military" Symphony and Beethoven's Ninth (finale) that these instruments joined the regular orchestra, and even then it was only on special occasions until well into the nineteenth century and almost never in German symphonic music.

In addition to the extra percussion, the use of a piccolo adds brilliance and an exotic shrillness to the orchestra's top. You can hear all this in the Chorus of Janissaries, "Singt dem grossen Bassa Lieder" (No. 5), which you will find on track 9 of the accompanying CD. Although less than two minutes long, this striking chorus tells you all you need to know about the special sound world that Mozart created for his Turkish excursion, and the gusto with which he seized the opportunity. Further

#	Title	Orchestration (in Addition to Strings)							
	Act I	Piccolo	Flutes	Oboes	Clarinets	Bassoons	Horns	Trumpets	Timpani/Percussion
1	Aria: Hier soll ich dich				2	2	2		
2	Song and Duet: Wer ein Liebchen hat gefunden		1	2		2	2		
3	Aria: Solche hergelauf'ne Laffen	1		2		2	2	2	perc.
4	Aria: Konstanze! Konstanze!		1	1			1	2	
5	Chorus: Singt dem grossen Bassa Lieder	1		2	2	2	2	2	timp./perc.
6	Aria: Ach ich liebte			2	2	2	2		
7	Trio: Marsch, marsch, marsch!			2	2	2	2	2	timp.
	Act 2								
8	Aria: Durch Zärtlichkeit			strings only					
9	Duet: Ich gehe, doch rathe ich dir			2		2	2		
10	Recitative and Aria: Welcher Wechsel herrscht/Traurigkeit		2	2	2 basset horns	2	2		
11	Aria: Martern aller Arten		1	1	2	2	2	2	timp.
12	Aria: Welche Wonne		2			2	2		
13	Aria: Frisch zum Kampfe			2			2	2	timp.
14	Duet: Vivat Bachus	1	2	2	2	2		2	perc.
15	Aria: Wenn der Freude Thränen fliessen		2	2	2	2	2		
16	Quartet: Ach Belmonte!		2	2		2	2	2	timp.
	Act 3								
17	Aria: Ich baue ganz		2		2	2	2		
18	Romance: In Mohrenland			strings only, without basses					
19	Aria: Ha! Wie will ich triumphiren	1		2	2	2	2		
20	Recitative and Duet: Welch ein Geschick		2		2		2		
21a	Vaudeville: Nie werd' ich deine Huld verkennen		2	2		2	2		
21b	Chorus: Bassa Selim lebe lange	1		2		2	2	2	timp./perc.

Table of Individual Numbers and Orchestration

enhancing this remarkably colorful opera is the fact, as you can see from the table, that with one exception, no two numbers are scored for exactly the same forces.

That exception consists of two arias, "Ach ich liebte" (No. 6) in act 1, in which Konstanze tells of her suffering on being parted from her beloved, and "Wenn der Freude" (No. 15) in act 2, in which Belmonte sings of his joy in being reunited with her. Mozart would not have expected anyone to recognize this level of subtlety in what is, after all, essentially accompaniment (and separated by nearly an hour of intervening music and one intermission), but this sort of sensitivity is typical of him. Much more important are the constantly changing colors in the orchestra that ensure that, even subconsciously, one is always hearing something new, and it is this freshness that has kept the score alive, despite the fact that as with much musical comedy (then and now), the characters tend to be one-dimensional and the plot, to put it mildly, somewhat contrived (which is, after all, part of the fun).

Music and Characters

Overture

Singspiel offers little opportunity to create the kind of dramatic continuity found in Mozart's Italian operas, and it is perhaps for this reason, along with the desire to blow his audience away with his compositional brilliance from the very first note, that he seized on the opportunity to write one of his biggest overtures in ABA form with the B section practically an independent movement in a slower tempo. Additionally, the overture runs straight into the opening scene without pause, a practice Mozart exploited to even more powerful effect in *Don Giovanni*. The banging and crashing of the percussion in the fast outer sections, as compared with the gracious elegance of the middle, offers a capsule view of the "East meets West" conflict that lies at the heart of the drama, and perfectly prepares for the story to follow.

Konstanze

Sometime between receiving the initial commission for the opera in 1781 and its premiere a year later, Mozart decided to transform Konstanze from a cardboard symbol of eponymous virtue into a tragic heroine. The result has always been controversial. Some contend that giving her two huge arias in a row in act 2, totaling around eighteen minutes of music between them, upsets the dramatic structure. "Nonsense!" say others: there's no dramatic structure to upset. Both sides have a point, but everyone agrees that dramatically apt or not, Konstanze gets the best music, and for most listeners, this fact settles the question once and for all. Mozart was aware of this problem, admitting that he basically got carried away in writing "Marten aller Arten" (No. 11), Konstanze's act 2 vocal explosion.

Certainly one of the reasons that Mozart felt the need to enrich Konstanze's character stems from the fact that her act 1 aria, "Ach ich liebte" (No. 6), is a fairly conventional, if undoubtedly flashy and difficult, "entrance aria" for a well-equipped singer that expresses none of the sorrow that she claims she feels on being separated from her beloved (unless of course she's trying to put a good face on things for Pasha Selim, which is a bit of psychological subtlety completely alien to these characters and this work in general). And so shortly into act 2, Mozart lets her steal the show. The first aria, "Traurigkeit ward mir zum Lose" (No. 10), which can be translated as "Sorrow has become my fate," is so tragic that it's easy to imagine that Konstanze will kill herself immediately afterwards. The scoring is gorgeous, with much of the accompaniment given to the woodwinds (including the only appearance in the entire opera of the basset horns, lower-pitched members of the clarinet family). The woodwind section's lonely solos and isolated stabs of pain greatly amplify the feeling of black despair that saturates the music.

Misery, however, is not Konstanze's only emotional state. When threatened by the Pasha with "torture of every sort" (i.e., "Martern aller Arten"), she cuts loose with nine minutes of really heroic defiance (No. 11). This aria is actually a quadruple concerto movement for solo flute, oboe, violin, and cello, in addition to the voice. It has a huge orchestral introduction that goes on for a good couple of minutes, leaving the characters on stage with nothing to do but listen, and then Konstanze cranks it out in spades. The aria has three big sections (and you hear them more than once). First Konstanze is defiant, then (along with the instrumental soloists) she pleads for pity, and finally, in a quicker tempo, she dares the Pasha to do his worst and declares herself more than ready for death. His spoken reply, a slightly more poetic version of "Wow!," counts as one of the most unintentionally comic anticlimaxes in all of opera, but then, after one of the great soprano displays in the entire operatic literature, what is he supposed to say?

In style and expression, both of Konstanze's big act 2 arias belong to a different world altogether, that of opera seria, in which the characters are all kings, queens, mythical heroes, gods, and goddesses, and the emotions are all larger than life and accordingly expressed in lengthy arias full of superhuman vocal fireworks. Whether or not you believe that these two numbers work in context or sound as if Konstanze has wandered in from the wrong opera is very much a matter of personal taste. In the hands (or larynx) of a great singer, you can only listen and react as does Pasha Selim. One thing that is guaranteed in any Mozart opera: if it comes to a conflict between musical expression and any other value or quantity, music always wins.

Belmonte

Mozart was musically lucky in that the original singers of both Konstanze and Belmonte were excellent, and he wrote for them accordingly. Belmonte's first two arias, "Hier soll ich" and "Konstanze!" (Nos. 1 and 4), both in act 1, essentially express the same emotion: the yearning for Konstanze. They follow, in their scoring, a pattern that Mozart will repeat in the Countess's two arias in *The Marriage of Figaro*. The sweetly nostalgic tone of the clarinets in No. 1, Mozart's musical symbol for yearning, yields to the more plaintive timbre of the oboe in No. 4, deepening the music's expression of unhappy longing. Belmonte has no further solo numbers until he is reunited with Konstanze at the end of act 2, but then Mozart gives him a vocal marathon (two challenging arias separated by a big ensemble) as long and difficult, relatively speaking, as the one just heard from the female lead.

Mozart rewrote Belmonte's act 2 aria "Wenn der Freude" (No. 15) more than once, and it exists today in both long and short versions (lasting around four and six minutes, respectively). The problem he had was essentially the same as that of Konstanze's "Martern aller Arten": What is everyone to do while Belmonte sings at length of his happiness at having at last found Konstanze? To this extent a love duet might have been more appropriate, but at this point most Konstanzes are sorely in need of a break, and she has a lot to do in the upcoming quartet. So Mozart shortened the aria accordingly, which has the dual advantage of looking less ridiculous and sparing the tenor at least a little: either way, this is a very difficult piece to sing.

Immediately following this aria, Belmonte takes a major part in the act's concluding quartet, "Ach Belmonte!" (No. 16), which runs for more than ten minutes, and then after intermission (if there is one—act 3 is fairly short), he's on again for another six-plus minutes. That's a total of more than twenty minutes of nearly continuous singing, and even Wagner seldom asks for more. Belmonte's final aria, "Ich baue ganz" (No. 17), represents a fulfillment of the desire he first expressed back in act 1. Having found Konstanze, he places himself in love's hands. Mozart brings back the euphonious orchestration of Belmonte's opening aria, with clarinets instead of oboes, and now also with two flutes adding their special radiance and soft sweetness to this rapturous, moonlit interlude.

Osmin

The part of Osmin is what's known in the business as a *basso buffo,* or comic bass. He's all bluster and no bite (although the part requires a wide vocal range combined with lots of temperament), and Konstanze's companion Blonde easily gets the better of him in their various encounters. That said, he has a lot to sing, and he gets to have the most fun of anyone. He's the second character that the audience meets, singing a little folk song in a plaintive minor key about the joys of finding the right woman: "Wer ein Liebchen" (No. 2). This turns into a duet with Belmonte. Then Osmin immediately has a wonderful number with Turkish percussion, "Solche hergelauf'ne Laffen" (No. 3), in which he goes nuts—to leaping octaves in the vocal line—thinking about horrifying ways to kill Pedrillo, his fellow servant and archnemesis (and also a kidnapping victim like Konstanze and Blonde). Finally, he enjoys a fine gloat in act 3, "Ha! wie will ich" (No. 19), aided by a gleefully chirping piccolo, when he believes the lovers will be punished for attempting to escape.

Then there are the ensembles: the show-stopping trio "Marsch, marsch, marsch!" (No. 7) at the end of act 1, which Mozart deliberately intended to whip the audience into a Viennese frenzy; the very funny duet with Blonde, "Ich gehe" (No. 9) in act 2, in which he laments the boldness of European women and retreats in terror when she threatens to scratch his eyes out; and the duet with Pedrillo in act 2, "Vivat Bachus" (No. 14), that gives him the chance gradually to get drunk as it proceeds. It's a terrific part for a talented singing actor and a surefire applause winner. Osmin's brand of music, often deliberately simple or cartoonish, will return to quite different effect in *The Magic Flute,* principally in the half-sinister, half-comic character of Monostatos.

Blonde and Pedrillo

Mozart takes care to give this pair—also members of the comic contingent—attractive solos that don't steal the spotlight from Konstanze and Belmonte. For example, both have arias accompanied only by strings, devoid of serious emotional content. Blonde's act 2 opener, "Durch Zärtlichkeit" (No. 8), suggests that European women need to be charmed, and not bullied into submission. It perfectly describes her situation with Osmin, who wants her very badly, without telling the audience much about her as a person, aside from the flickers of defiant, stratospheric coloratura toward the aria's end (like Konstanze, only on a budget). Pedrillo's act 3 aria, "In Mohrenland" (No. 18), is a serenade-under-the-balcony-style ballad in which plucked strings imitate the sounds of the mandolin. He also has a short, militant aria in act 2, "Frisch zum Kampfe" (No. 13), requiring a very powerful voice to cut through the heavy orchestration, as he screws up his courage to implement the escape plan. Immediately thereafter he enjoys the happy task of getting Osmin drunk in the duet "Vivat Bachus."

In his later operas, Mozart takes great pains to flesh out even the secondary characters: think of Marcellina and Bartolo in

Figaro or Zerlina and Masetto in *Don Giovanni.* Putting the entire cast on an almost equal footing is one of the many things that makes the ensuing works so rich and diverse, but it also makes them longer (although not as long as many of Mozart's own earlier operas), because such treatment inevitably takes time. It's clear from his handling of Belmonte and Konstanze that Mozart was still testing the waters, trying to see how much opera seria–style emotional force he could infuse into a comedy with spoken words, and so he wisely decided to draw Blonde and Pedrillo more to scale and observe the conventions of his time. But in his very last opera, *The Magic Flute,* Mozart finally did create a singspiel in which every character gets full musical consideration.

Pasha Selim

This is a speaking role, which is a good thing, because it means that the Pasha's motivations and feelings remain mysterious. So the transformation from someone threatening Konstanze with torture of all kinds to the magnanimous liberator of the lovers at the end of the opera never really comes into question, lacking as it does further musical definition. The Pasha, in short, belongs entirely to the admittedly artificial mechanics of the plot. Making a musical character out of him would have necessarily meant at least a couple of arias and ensembles, and so, in turn, a much longer opera with a consequent loss of focus on the "good guys." In the relatively black-and-white world of musical comedy, nothing so effectively dramatizes the opposition of the two sides better than giving this character no music at all.

The Abduction from the Seraglio is clearly a transitional work, full of great music but also a bit at odds with itself. The best musical moments essentially stand outside the world of singspiel and risk overwhelming the more conventional numbers. In his later operas, working alongside an excellent librettist, Mozart would learn the secret of developing his characters gradually, over the course of the entire work, rather than all at once in a long series of action-stopping arias. The length of the arias themselves would shrink, again providing for greater dramatic continuity. Long tracts of continuous music would come to typify the marvelously extended and exciting finales, which simultaneously advance the action and reveal character and emotion. In *The Magic Flute,* Mozart will in turn take the lessons learned in both opera seria and his Italian comedies and apply them to the medium of singspiel, creating a unique work quite unlike anything else. But he's not there yet.

Even so, it would be a mistake to consider *The Abduction* in any way immature, just as it would *Idomeneo.* This is, after all, Mozart's tenth completed opera. By this time, there was no composer that could touch him in vividness of musical characterization, not to mention the sheer color and variety that he lavished on each score. If his natural bigness of vision sits uncomfortably at times with the scale of the medium, then it's certainly a fault in the right direction, and already one can see several traits that will be developed further in *The Marriage of Figaro.* These include the emphasis on sympathetic, intelligent female characters; the subtle use of a large orchestra (woodwinds in particular) to consistently color the emotional content of each aria; and the willingness to write very serious music within the larger context of comedy. This last quality is perhaps the most important of all. Because of it, Mozart was able to elevate comic opera beyond the superficial and the trivial, and turn it instead into an expression of the sincere emotions and feelings of believable characters.

Le Nozze di Figaro (The Marriage of Figaro)
1786

Introduction

*T*he *Marriage of Figaro* is the first of Mozart's operas with words by Lorenzo Da Ponte, one of the more remarkable characters of his day (he was half Jewish; a sometime priest; and a notorious womanizer, poet, adventurer, and full-time opportunist, who eventually ended his career in New York City teaching Italian literature at Columbia University). The relationship between the two men represents a high point in the history of opera, and the three works that they created together were true collaborations, in which text and musical setting fit together with a naturalness and inevitability seldom equaled since. Da Ponte's libretto is an adaptation of a French play by Beaumarchais, in fact the sequel to the same author's *The Barber of Seville.*

    The Marriage of Figaro was banned in Vienna for its scandalous portrayal of a decadent (and stupid) aristocracy, so it was something of a miracle for Da Ponte to obtain permission from Emperor Joseph II to produce an operatic version. Although some of the more offensive elements were eliminated, what remains is hardly flattering to the nobility, although this may in fact have figured in the emperor's plans. Joseph II was an "enlightened" monarch, which in practice meant suppression of the power of the Catholic Church, freedom for the serfs, stricter control over his noble vassals, and marginally greater social tolerance and intellectual freedom. He seemed to take a personal interest in *Figaro,* even to the extent of attending the dress rehearsal in April of 1786, an almost unheard of act of patronage.

Although it is structured in four acts, it's almost easier to see the opera as falling into two halves, each of which culminates in a grand finale (that of act 2 is discussed in detail in "Mozart's Operatic Style"). In fact, all of Mozart's subsequent operas would adopt the two-act format, which must have appealed to his finely tuned sense of balance and symmetry. This may seem like a technical point, but it has a direct consequence in terms of the opera's stageworthiness, for many comic operas of the day featured a three-act design, with the last part consisting of a very short, superficial, throw-away resolution to the plot, almost deliberately designed to trivialize the significance of the action.

How different is *Figaro*! For the very first time in a comic opera, the composer takes his characters as seriously as they take themselves. Despite the lunacy of the climactic garden scene, the emotional states of the principals come across as very real, and the sublime (no other word will do) moment in which the Countess restores order and grants forgiveness to her husband, and by extension to all concerned, is the lynchpin that only at the very last moment completes Mozart's ongoing sketch of her character. Even more importantly, the resolution of the drama does not come about by some improbable or purely mechanical working of the plot imposed from without, but rather through a conscious act of grace on the part of the single character (as Mozart's music has already revealed) capable of rising to the occasion. For this reason, the Countess remains one of the most moving and believable personalities ever achieved in music.

Here, then, is the essence of Mozart's famous rejoinder to the "too many notes" criticism: there truly are only as many as

#	Title	Flutes	Oboes	Clarinets	Bassoons	Horns	Trumpets	Timpani
	Le Nozze di Figaro: Quick Reference							
				Orchestration (in Addition to Strings)				
	Act I							
1	Duettino: Cinque, diece, venti	2	2		2	2		
2	Duettino: Se a caso madama la notte	2	2		2	2		
3	Cavatina: Se vuol ballare, signor contino		2		2	2		
4	Aria: La vendetta, oh la vendetta	2	2		2	2	2	yes
5	Duettino: Via resti servita	2	2		2	2		
6	Aria: Non sò più cosa son, cosa faccio			2	2	2		
7	Terzetto: Cosa sento		2	2	2	2		
8	Chorus: Giovani liete, fiori spargete	2			2	2		
9	Aria: Non più andrai, farfallone amoroso	2	2		2	2	2	yes
	Act 2							
10	Cavatina: Porgi amor qualche ristoro			2	2	2		
11	Arietta: Voi che sapete	1	1	1	1	2		
12	Aria: Venite, inginocchiatevi	2	2		2	2		
13	Trio: Susanna, or via sortite		2		2	2		
14	Duettino: Aprite presto, aprite			strings only				
15	Finale: Esci omai, garzon malnato	2	2	2	2	2	2	yes
	Act 3							
16	Duettino: Crudel, perchè finora fermi	2			2	2		
17	Recitative & Aria: Hai già vinta/Vedrò, mentr'io	2	2		2	2	2	yes
18	Sestetto: Riconosci in questo amplesso	2	2		2	2		
19	Recitative & Aria: E Susanna non vien/Dove sono		2		2	2		
20	Duettino: Che soave zeffiretto		1		1			
21	Chorus: Ricevete, o padroncina	1	2		1	2		
22	Finale: Ecco la marcia, andiamo	2	2	2	2	2	2	yes
	Act 4							
23	Cavatina: L'ho perduta, me meschina			strings only				
24	Aria: Il capro, è la capretta			strings only				
25	Aria: In quegli anni, in cui val poco	1		2	2	2		
26	Recitative & Aria: Tutto e disposto: l'ora dovrebbe/Aprite un po'			2	2	2		
27	Recitative & Aria: Giunse alfin il momento/Deh, vieni	1	1		1			
28	Finale: Pian pianin, le andro piu presso	2	2	2	2	2	2	yes

Table of Individual Numbers and Orchestration

are necessary, because he stays with his characters and lets them continue to develop up to the very last bar. Despite the inevitable stops and starts attendant on the division of the opera into recitative and aria, the overall impression is of an integrated whole in which character and action function harmoniously and organically in achieving the final resolution. It is perhaps for this reason that Mozart and Da Ponte called *Figaro* a *dramma giocoso* (cheerful drama) rather than an opera buffa, and in fact never used this more common term at all to describe their work together. The appellation *dramma giocoso* was not unique to them, but in their case, it truly means what it says.

Music and Characters

Overture

One of Mozart's most famous pieces and a popular concert opener to this very day, the overture to *The Marriage of Figaro* quotes no themes from the opera, but perfectly establishes the mood of madcap comedy. It seems to start, like the story itself, in midstream, as its opening phrases tumble over one another in a rush to the first great outburst, while the coda, in march tempo, subtly hints at the conclusion of the first act.

Figaro

Mozart gives Figaro three arias, and since two of these occur in the first act, his character naturally dominates and sets the scene for what comes later. His first aria, "Si vuol ballare" (No. 3), establishes him at once as a clever servant and a "smooth operator." The triple-time and minuet tempo neatly illustrate the challenge he throws out to the count: "If you want to dance, you'll do it to my tune," while prominent horns and oboes give the music a rustic, folksy quality that proclaims Figaro as a commoner, an instantly likeable, self-assured everyman.

His second aria, the famous "Non più andrai" (No. 9 and track 10 on the included CD), is important in several respects. It is the only aria that actually concludes an act. Mozart highlights the mock military character with ample use of trumpets and drums, both supporting the meaning of the words and also creating a natural climax guaranteed to bring down the curtain to a storm of applause. The tune, one of the catchiest in the opera (and indeed among the most famous in all of Mozart, which means in all of music), similarly has a deliberately popular flavor, and it contrasts very strongly with Figaro's first number. The physicality of these two arias—one a dance, the other a march—completes the illustration of the character's (and the opera's) masculine side, and creates the strongest possible contrast to the opening of the second act, which will be all about the women.

Figaro's third aria, "Aprite un po'" (No. 26) in act 4, adds depth to his character by permitting the audience to see him angry and wounded. It has been said, speaking strictly from the point of view of plot, that his readiness to believe himself betrayed by Susanna doesn't make him look especially smart and isn't consistent with his know-it-all cleverness. But even if true (and it's debatable), that's not really the point. What matters is that the music fleshes him out as a person, gives an added twist to the "battle of the sexes" subplot, and makes him, and thus the entire opera, more credible. It's also worth noting, in conclusion, that each of his arias is scored differently, and you will see that Mozart invariably takes great pains to provide as much instrumental variety as he does emotional contrast.

The Countess

If Figaro represents confidence and gaiety, the Countess is his emotional opposite. Melancholy, languishing for want of love, but graceful and dignified despite it all, hers is the character that provides the opera's expressive heart, and it's the presence of her dignity and decency that elevates the comedy to the level of human drama that we, as listeners, come to care about. I have already discussed in detail her first aria, "Porgi amor" (CD track 1) in "Mozart's Operatic Style." The depth of her wistful longing becomes truly manifest in her second aria, "Dove sono" (No. 19), which forms the emotional core of act 3 and occupies a position at its exact center. Once again Mozart scores the aria differently than previously, and here the replacement of clarinets with the plaintive timbre of the oboes gives a more bitter edge to the Countess's misery. I have already mentioned the wonderful moment at the end of act 4 where she forgives the Count for his follies and shows herself to be as classy and poised in victory as she is in despair.

There's one more quality worth pointing out about the Countess, and Mozart reveals it most obviously in her vivacious scenes with Susanna: she is still a very young woman (only about twenty). Her poise and self-control often make audiences think that she is much older, but although she may be emotionally very mature, she is not only a girl who feels the pain of rejection very, very acutely, but she still has plenty of playfulness and fight inside of her, and the role needs to be played accordingly. Her youth makes the exchange of clothing and identity in act 4 with Susanna, her maid, entirely plausible, just as it makes the Count's behavior towards her appear even more obnoxious and incomprehensible.

Susanna

Susanna is the Countess's alter-ego, in a sense, showing much of the vivacity and high spirits of the Rosina of *The Barber of Seville*. Indeed, the two of them together define the full range of womanly emotion and virtue (and it's a much more flattering portrait than the male side receives). Mozart takes great pains to permit Susanna's character to emerge very slowly. At first, she is seen primarily in duets and ensembles with just about everyone in the opera, and her presence brightens and energizes the music like a ray of sunshine. Her first aria, "Venite, inginocchiatevi" (No. 12 in act 2), is a charming, comic "action piece" in which she chatters away while dressing Cherubino as a woman.

Her great moment, however, comes in the act 4 aria "Deh, vieni" (No. 27), where the audience hears some of the yearning that was hitherto the exclusive province of the Countess (although without any trace of sadness). The sensuous use of solo woodwinds curling around the vocal line adds immeasurably to the music's evocation of a woman in love, although the simplicity of the tune, with its *pizzicato* (plucked) string accompaniment, reveals Susanna, like Figaro, to be one of the common folk. Even more importantly, this aria, which occurs just before the opera's big finale, represents the culmination of what has been a gradual and very skillfully planned shift in the opera's emotional center of gravity, from the world of the men (as represented by Figaro, Bartolo, and the Count in act 1) to that of the women.

Finally, this aria confirms Susanna's significance as arguably the prime mover of the entire opera. It is the count's desire for her that sets the story in motion, and her cleverness (she's much smarter than Figaro) keeps the plot moving on towards its ultimate happy resolution. By the end of the opera, she has, in a series of duets and ensembles, foiled the Count, restored her mistress's happiness, gotten her man, and except for a single momentary lapse (when she sees Figaro embracing Marcellina without knowing that the older woman is in fact his mother), she has never wavered in her resolve or constancy. "Deh vieni," the last aria in the opera, is Mozart's gift to her, a reward that in sheer lyrical beauty elevates her to the stature of the Countess in terms of nobility and grace, even as the music itself confirms that she is still one of us.

The Count

Almaviva is basically an incredible jerk. His single aria, "Vedrò, mentr'io" (No. 17), which occurs towards the beginning of act 3, expresses his fear of being made a fool of by his servants and his desire to have his revenge. As with the character of Osmin in *The Abduction from the Seraglio,* Mozart expresses baritonal rage through wild leaps in the vocal line. All of the principal adult male characters get arias scored with the masculine sound of trumpets and drums, but this one does not recall Figaro's "Non più andrai" as much as it does Bartolo's vengeance aria, "La vendetta," heard earlier in act 1. Contrast is all-important here, for the very next aria heard, after the intervening sextet, is the Countess's "Dove sono," making the comparison between husband and wife particularly vivid.

Otherwise, Mozart defines the Count's jerkishness in a series of ensembles, and in particular through his interactions with Susanna, whom he ineptly keeps trying to seduce throughout the opera, finally settling on a sleazy bargain, "Crudel! Perchè finora" (No. 16), in which he agrees to give Susanna money to pay off Figaro's debt to Marcellina in exchange for sex, which he of course he equates with true love. His humiliation at the end of act 4 is thus all the more satisfying (and pathetic), and the

Countess's forgiveness even more impressive, given what Mozart reveals about him, although one can't help but wonder how sincere his repentance actually is.

Cherubino

A horny young boy on the verge of manhood who lusts after every female in the opera, Cherubino's very innocence and directness offends the Count, who is, after all, basically engaged in the same sort of chase, but who finds the page's stark emotional honesty (never mind the competition) absurdly threatening. The part is what's called in the opera business a *trouser role,* meaning a male role intended to be sung by a female performer. Cherubino is a one-dimensional character for the obvious reason that he only has one thing on his mind, but it's interesting that both of his arias, "Non so più" and "Voi che sapete" (Nos. 6 and 11), concern the desire for love, and both have clarinets, as does the Countess's "Porgi amor."

There seems little doubt that Mozart here associated the mellow tone of the clarinet with the lovelorn emotional state of these characters, although it won't do to make a fetish out of this point. Both Figaro (No. 26) and Basilio (No. 25) have them in act 4 in very different expressive contexts. Their tone in Cherubino's music is what Verdi would have called a *tinta,* or color, that shades the listener's perception of the vocal line and gently reinforces the feelings of the characters.

Bartolo, Basilio, and Marcellina

The characters of Bartolo and Marcellina belong together, not just because Mozart and Da Ponte conceived them as a pair to begin with, but because they undergo exactly the same metamorphosis, switching sides from the Count's to Figaro's (whose parents they turn out to be). Bartolo's vigorous vengeance aria, "La vendetta" (No. 4), establishes him as a nasty old fool, and with its trumpets and drums, it reinforces the masculine character of the opening act. Marcellina's aria "Il capro" (No. 24) has a similar function, musically speaking. It represents the feminine counterpart of Bartolo's, and it reinforces the battle-of-the-sexes opposition of blustering men vs. suffering women. Its scoring, for strings only, is rather plain, as befits a plain and somewhat old-fashioned character, but the moral point that it makes (that even in the animal kingdom, males treat their females better than men treat women) couldn't be more vivid, and it critically establishes act 4 as essentially belonging to the women, who are, at last, entirely united in sentiment in opposition to the men.

Basilio's act 4 aria, "In quegli anni" (No. 25), like Marcellina's, is often cut in performance (and on some recordings) so as to speed up the action and head into the finale more quickly. This is a mistake for several reasons, not the least of which is that both these arias deal broadly with the subject of people behaving like fools and mistreating each other. The message they deliver when heard in tandem is very cynical: if we do not wish to suffer (says Marcellina), we must avoid emotional entanglements entirely (says Basilio). Figaro's ensuing rant against women, "Aprite un po'," offers Marcellina's observations from the male perspective, but with the crucial difference that Figaro is mistaken in his beliefs, and together these three arias define the opera's basic conflict in more universal terms.

But Mozart immediately counterbalances these thoughts with Susana's "Deh vieni," telling us that the need for love remains as strong as ever. There's something wonderful about the contrast here: for a moment, Mozart lets Marcellina, Basilio, and Figaro step outside the drama for a bitter, three-pronged reflection on the human condition, before Susana returns to the opera's main plot by expressing her own personal feelings—making her all the more human and sympathetic as a result. All told, this sequence of arias in act 4 perfectly sets up the madcap antics of the finale, offering a chance to pause, take a deep breath, and summarize all that we have seen so far and ponder its larger significance, before the contingencies of the plot drive irresistibly forward to the happy conclusion.

Barbarina

The gardener Antonio's young daughter Barbarina has a single short aria that opens act 4, "L'ho perduta" (No. 23), in which she laments the loss of a pin. The music is truly tragic—indeed, it represents the darkest moment in the entire opera—and therein resides its humor: the contrast between subject and musical setting couldn't be more amusing. But at a deeper level, no single part of the opera more tellingly reveals Mozart's acuity of emotional insight than this tiny two minutes of music. The aria is tragic not just for reasons of comedy but because Barbarina is truly emotionally devastated by her loss. So Mozart lets the audience experience her distress as *she* feels it, and not as he, a disinterested observer, judges or interprets it. There is no greater testament to his commitment to psychological realism than his willingness to let the characters be themselves, nor is there a more impressive example than this of Mozart's gift for allowing his characters to reveal who they are through the music that they sing.

These, then, constitute the principle participants in Mozart's *dramma giocoso,* and although you will spend some two and half hours listening to the entire work, I think you will agree that when all is said and done, the music comes across as astonishingly punctual. Indeed, accuracy and efficiency are two of Mozart's hallmarks. They would have to be, considering the fact that he is trying to present fully developed characters who are restricted to no more than two or three arias in the entire work (plus some ensembles and the two big finales), and even those arias seldom last more than three or four minutes apiece.

Indeed, the length of the work is determined more by the number of characters receiving the full Mozartean treatment than by the amount of music that they actually sing. Also keep in mind that these purely musical considerations had to take into account as well the wishes of the singers and their vocal capabilities, the logistics of rehearsal and performance, and various other local circumstances. In the world of eighteenth-century opera, the composer's score and intentions were hardly sacrosanct. That Mozart was able to create a work of such consistency and emotional truth given these constraints is one of the great highwire acts in all of music, and something of a miracle, but it's one that he would repeat several times over in the works to come.

Don Giovanni
1787

Introduction

The Marriage of Figaro was not a success in Vienna, where court intrigues combined with its musical complexity to brand the work as "difficult." It took Prague by storm, though, and it was because of its overwhelmingly favorable reception there that we have both the "Prague" Symphony (No. 38) and *Don Giovanni,* which was composed expressly for that singularly musical city and first performed at the Estates Theater on October 29, 1787. It's been playing in that same house pretty much continuously ever since, probably making it the longest-running show in history, and you can see it there even today. For the Vienna premiere in 1788, Mozart made some revisions, replacing Don Ottavio's act 2 aria "Il mio tesoro" (No. 21) with act 1's "Dalla sua pace" (No. 10a) and writing a new duet for Zerlina and Leporello (No. 21a) and an additional aria for Donna Elvira, the famous "Mi tradì" (No. 21b). In modern performances, both of Don Ottavio's arias are usually included along with Elvira's, while the duet (which was supposed to provide additional comic relief) is omitted.

I have discussed how Mozart and Da Ponte did not call *The Marriage of Figaro* an opera buffa (comic opera) but rather a *dramma giocoso,* or "cheerful drama." *Don Giovanni* proves once and for all that this distinction really does mean something for them (if not necessarily for others), as there's more of the drama and less of the comic here than in any other mature stage work by Mozart. Virtually a study in masochistic obsession, the opera's psychological complexities have inspired numerous commentaries and continue to provide endless opportunities for scholarly debate, imaginative stage direction (for better or for worse), and thoughtful singing actors.

All of the characters are damaged in some way. Donna Anna, who has just lost her father, doesn't seem to care much for her suitor Don Ottavio at all, a fact that he simply refuses to notice with his repeated demands that they marry immediately. Donna Elvira, a hysterical stalker, is crazily obsessed with Don Giovanni before the opera even begins. What makes her even crazier is the fact that she actually loves him. The peasant girl, Zerlina, asks for the forgiveness of her oafish boyfriend, Masetto (for almost cheating on him with you-know-who), by challenging him to beat her and scratch her eyes out. Indeed, the level of violence and cruelty in this opera is both astonishing and shockingly casual. Witness this utterly typical bit of recitative from the very first scene of act 1:

DON GIOVANNI: Leporello, where are you?

LEPORELLO: I'm here, alas. And you?

DG: I'm here.

L: Who is dead? You, or the old man?

DG: Such a ridiculous question! The old man.

L: Congratulations. Two impressive achievements! Forcing yourself on the daughter, and then murdering the father.

DG: He asked for it, and it's his problem.

L: And Donna Anna—she asked for it too?

DG: (moving to hit L) Shut up. Don't make me angry. Come along, unless you want the same treatment.

#	Title	Flutes	Oboes	Clarinets	Bassoons	Horns	Trumpets	Timpani	Trombones	Extras
	Don Giovanni: Quick Reference — Orchestration (in Addition to Strings)									
	Act 1									
1	Introduction: Notte e giorno faticar	2	2		2	2				
2	Recitative & Duet: Ma qual mai s'offre, oh Dei	2	2		2	2				
3	Aria/Trio: Ah chi mi dice mai			2	2	2				
4	Aria: Madamina, il catalogo è questo	2	2		2	2				
5	Chorus: Giovinette che fate all'amore	2	2		2	2				
6	Aria: Ho capito, Signor	2			2	2				
7	Duettino: Là ci darem la mano	1	2		2	2				
8	Aria: Ah fuggi il traditor				strings only					
9	Quartet: Non ti fidar	1		2	2	2				
10	Recitative & Aria: Or sai chi l'onore	2	2		2	2	2			
10a	Aria: Dalla sua pace	1	2		2	2				
11	Aria: Fin ch'han dal vino	2	2	2	2	2				
12	Aria: Batti, batti	1	1		1	2				
13	Finale: Presto, presto	2	2	2	2	2	2	Yes		3 small orchestras onstage
	Act 2									
14	Duet: Eh via buffone		2			2				
15	Trio: Ah taci	2		2	2	2				
16	Canzonetta: Deh vieni alla finestra				strings					mandolin
17	Aria: Metà di voi	2	2		2	2				
18	Aria: Vedrai, carino	2		2	2	2				
19	Sextet: Sola, sola	2	2	2	2	2	2	Yes		
20	Aria: Ah pietà, Signori	2			2	2				
21	Aria: Il mio tesoro			2	2	2				
21a	Duet: Per queste tue manine	2	2		2	2				
21b	Recitative & Aria: Mi tradì	1		1	1	2				
22	Duet: O statua gentilissima	2			2	2				wind band (w/ trombones) in recitative
23	Recitative & Aria: Non mi dir	1		2	2	2				
24	Finale: Già la mensa	2	2	2	2	2	2	Yes	3	wind band onstage

Table of Individual Numbers and Orchestration

From this point on, hardly a scene goes by in which someone is not beaten, threatened with violence, or emotionally tortured. Act 1 begins with the attempted rape of Donna Anna and murder of her father, and closes with the attempted rape of Zerlina. In act 2 Masetto shows up with a posse intent on clobbering Don Giovanni, only to find himself beaten in turn. Everyone, including his boss, threatens to kill Leporello on multiple occasions. Relative peace can only be restored when the source of all of this chaos, Don Giovanni himself, is sucked down to hell in the ultimate act of self-destruction set to the most hair-raising music that Mozart ever composed. And all of this in what is purportedly a comedy!

In fact, much of the opera really is humorous, albeit in a warped sort of way. Many of the situations are inherently comical, not the least of which is that for a supposed "suave womanizer," everything that the Don tries to do (including staying alive) ends in failure. His sidekick, Leporello, provides an undercurrent of cynical and amusing chatter that acts as a counterpoise to even the most deeply serious scenes. Comedy is one of three factors that make the drama easier to accept. A second factor is the element of the supernatural, which puts a little distance between the spectator and the characters, never asking us as audience members quite to believe that (in retrospect) the situations we have witnessed could actually be real. For Mozart takes his characters very seriously indeed, and so believable does he make them that we don't even blink when suddenly, late in the opera, we are confronted with a talking statue and a chorus of demons dragging Don Giovanni to hell. In the final scene, everyone on stage nonchalantly accepts this as perfectly normal, announces their future plans, and moves on. We take our cues from them; we accept it as well.

The music, which so easily accommodates and makes vivid this fantastic element, is the third and most important factor drawing us into the opera's disturbing world. Mozart seduces us into accepting as genuine the emotions of these strange, obsessive, and deranged people. What makes the opera so powerful is the tension Mozart creates in arousing our sympathies for characters who are often insensitive, self-obsessed, manipulative, or deluded, despite the fact that their frequently awful behavior evokes our instinctive feelings of revulsion. Achieving this kind of strong, almost visceral bond of empathy between a character (however vile) and the audience is one of those things that music can do more effectively than any other medium in a dramatic context. Latter-day composers from Richard Strauss (*Salome*) to Dmitri Shostakovich (*Lady Macbeth of Mtsensk*) have exploited this to singular advantage, but Mozart was the first to discover this quality and use it successfully.

In this respect, *Don Giovanni* is a remarkably modern conception. You will not find any opera of similar depth starring an antihero either in the work of Mozart's contemporaries or predecessors (Monteverdi's *The Coronation of Poppea* is perhaps the one noteworthy exception). Among later composers, Wagner never asks his audience to sympathize with or look kindly upon his "bad guys," and he certainly never wrote a whole opera about one. In the twentieth century, in addition to the Strauss and Shostakovich operas already mentioned, Benjamin Britten's *Peter Grimes,* Leos Janácek's *From the House of the Dead,* and Berg's *Wozzeck* are perhaps the most famous contemporary works celebrating the humanity of characters who would, in earlier periods, have been considered unworthy of appearing on the operatic stage. All of these marvelous creations owe some measure of debt to the example of *Don Giovanni.*

Modern, too, is the often cinematic pacing. The overture, which establishes the opposite poles of supernatural terror and madcap comedy, runs directly into the first scene without pause. Each of the two acts contains several scene changes, with the momentum picking up as the opera heads into the large tracts of continuous music that comprise the two finales. Act 1, as you can see below, contains two changes of scene in its last two numbers, while act 2 has four changes of scene in its last five numbers:

Act 1

- A garden at night, in front of Donna Anna's house (Nos. 1 and 2)
- The street at night, towards dawn (Nos. 3–11)
- A park outside Don Giovanni's palace (No. 12—part 1 of No. 13)
- Don Giovanni's ballroom, lit up for a grand party (part 2 of No. 13)

Act 2

- The street outside an inn, towards evening (Nos. 14–18)
- The courtyard of Donna Anna's house (Nos. 19–21b)
- A churchyard with equestrian statues (No. 22)
- A dark room in Donna Anna's house (No. 23)
- A banquet hall in Don Giovanni's house (No. 24)

Mozart's use of the orchestra reflects his desire to build tension steadily. Note that in both acts, but for a single exception in each, trumpets and/or timpani appear only in the finales, along with the most complex and lavish orchestral apparatus Mozart was ever to employ: three stage bands in act 1 and, in act 2, an onstage wind ensemble in addition to three trombones in the orchestra (instruments musically associated with solemn religious rituals or supernatural occurrences in Mozart's day). And yet the two acts are also subtly differentiated. Despite even more lavish use of the full woodwind section than in *Figaro,* the plaintive sound of the oboes dominates in act 1, while the more seductive and emotionally expressive clarinets take over in act 2. Mozart even makes a charming little joke out of this fact in the finale. There, the onstage wind band entertains Don Giovanni with tunes from three popular operas of the day. The first two selections, not by Mozart, feature oboes, while "Non più andrai" from *The Marriage of Figaro* kicks in third, as a solo for the two clarinets—a Mozartean fingerprint as instantly recognizable as any leitmotif of Wagner's.

As in the previous opera, the use of clarinets, bassoons, and horns together (now sometimes with flutes as well) often expresses sadness or longing. It's interesting to note, however, that in the Vienna version of the opera, where Mozart replaced Don Ottavio's second-act aria "Il mio tesoro" with "Dalla sua pace" in act 1, he retained that act's characteristic wind timbre favoring the oboes, which is logical since the music arises in reaction to Donna Anna's previous aria and so shares a similar instrumental setting (not to mention a text that says that Don Ottavio's entire life is but a reflection of Donna Anna's). In act 2, on the other hand, both Ottavio's and Anna's arias sport clarinets, thus preserving a similar connection between them, but in this new and different context. These are not details that are necessarily supposed to strike you forcibly, or even consciously, but they're worth noting all the same for what they reveal about the relationships between character, aria, and the instrumental cast of the whole act.

Within the ever-changing orchestral fabric from one number to the next, Mozart creates unity by "coloring" each act in a consistent manner, while at the same time applying his special gift of bringing to life through music a truly remarkable, even bizarre, array of personalities. The contrast with *Figaro* couldn't be greater. In that opera, even the bad guys have their amiable side, or else they at least appear amusingly foolish. *Don Giovanni,* however, is without doubt its predecessor's evil twin: no one is amiable for long, and everyone (save perhaps Zerlina and Mesetto) is at some point absolutely frightening, whether as a result of insanity, cruelty, insensitivity, or simple nameless perversity.

Music and Characters

Overture

As noted, and also as in *The Abduction from the Seraglio,* the overture runs into the opera's first scene without pause. But the most important thing about it is that it begins with the terrifying music representing the living statue of the Commendatore coming to dine with *Don Giovanni* in the finale of act 2. All of the music of this slow introduction will return, with enriched scoring (three trombones) and with the actual vocal lines superimposed on top. No composer before Mozart had ever attempted to create and sustain this kind of dramatic tension, in effect asking a musical question from the very first note (What does this frightening outburst mean?) and withholding the answer until more than two hours later.

How brilliantly this gambit pays off! It creates suspense exactly as Alfred Hitchcock used to define it: the audience knows the killer with the knife is just around the corner, while the victim is oblivious to the danger. It then becomes the job of the filmmaker to tease his audience, delaying the fatal encounter to the last possible nerve-wracking moment. Indeed, this opening suggests tragedy, not comedy, to follow, and when the humorous allegro begins in stark opposition to the overture's initial few minutes, it at once establishes the emotional ambiguity that Mozart and Da Ponte will so brilliantly exploit throughout the remainder of the work. From here on, the audience knows that terror is lurking somewhere out there but does not know what form it will take or when it will strike. When it finally does, since its music has been heard before, it not only has all of its original explosive power, it adds an equally devastating quality only manifest in witnessing a terrible destiny, at last fulfilled.

Donna Anna

In some ways Donna Anna is the opera's most intriguing character. Is she an archetypical noblewoman who does and says all the right things, or is she dissembling? The evidence is mixed. The audience eventually learns that she's already put off her wedding to Don Ottavio several times, and when he wants to know if the ceremony is still on for the day after her father's murder, one can only agree with her outraged reaction. But in the great accompanied recitative leading up to her first aria, "Or sai chi l'onore" (No. 10), she lets slip the interesting fact that she only began to struggle against the mysterious stranger in her bedroom after he had embraced her and she realized that it was not Ottavio.

That, anyway, is what she tells him, but what else could a theoretically virtuous aristocratic woman say? Was Anna in fact expecting her nocturnal visitor, and is her relationship to Don Ottavio all that propriety suggests it should be? Consider, for example, the fact that as the opera opens, it is Don Giovanni who is trying to get away from Donna Anna and not the other way around (although that is how she makes it appear when she describes the scene to Don Ottavio). When Don Ottavio attempts to comfort her, she lashes out at him in fury, screaming, "Leave me, cruel one, leave me!," and then a moment later looks at him in surprise and recovers her composure, telling him, "It's you . . . forgive me . . . my darling . . . my grief, the pain . . . ." She then has Ottavio take an oath of vengeance against the murderer of her father (reinforced by the blatant appeal to his honor in her first aria).

Certainly there's more going on here than meets the eye, particularly when in her magnificent second-act aria, the rondo "Non mi dir" (No. 23), Donna Anna effectively tells Don Ottavio that until the vengeance business gets resolved, she certainly will never consider marrying him. The word *rondo* means different things (musically speaking) in different contexts; in "Non mi dir" it signifies an aria in two contrasting tempos, first slow, then faster. The setting perfectly compliments the text as regards the slow section, particularly the turn to a sad minor key at the words "Calm your anguish, lest I yearn to die of grief!" But when the tempo increases and Anna sings "Perhaps one day heaven will once again take pity on me," the tone is cheerful, the voice borne aloft on flights of elaborate coloratura. She leaves Don Ottavio (to whom the aria is addressed) to music quite different from the affected concern for his feelings with which it began.

Three points at least are clear: Donna Anna has confidence in her future, she is thinking primarily of herself, and the music reveals this in a most emphatic way. On the other hand, the possibility can't be discounted that the soprano who originally sang the role threatened to quit unless she got a show-stopping conclusion to her big act 2 aria. For while it's certainly fun applying a little imagination to the discussion of this or any other Mozart character, it's also worth cautioning against overintellectualizing and trying to find deep meaning in every detail. It never pays to forget that Mozart was at all times a tremendously practical and experienced musician adapting to all kinds of awkward and specific local circumstances. When all is said and done, great music remains its own justification, whatever additional significance may be found in it.

However you choose to look at Donna Anna, the character works equally well played either subtle or "straight." That's the beauty of Mozart's music too: it supports a variety of interpretations. Anna's strength of will pales somewhat in comparison to

Donna Elvira, who is simply crazy and therefore often more obviously vivid and fun to watch (but then, a manipulative schemer
must necessarily be a more shadowy figure than a lunatic whose
emotions all lie on the surface). In any event, the murder of
Anna's father, the result of Don Giovanni's attempt to get away
from her, sets the plot of the opera in motion, and it is she who,
Don Ottavio in tail, leads the cast in pursuit of him for the next
two acts. Aside from her solo arias, she plays a major role in all
of the important ensembles, and like Susanna in *The Marriage of
Figaro,* her character provides the focus around which the various
strands of plot intertwine. And also like Susanna, she gets the
last aria in the opera before the big finale.

Don Ottavio

Don Ottavio is a wimp, but one with a great sense of honor and
gentlemanly breeding. He spends the entire opera lying bodily
across the great puddle of life, figuratively speaking, so that
Donna Anna won't get her dainty feet wet as she walks across
it (and him). By his own admission in act 2 (in the recitative
before "Non mi dir"), he's been in this position for some time.
But that doesn't matter, because Don Ottavio is in love to the
point of inanity, or more properly speaking, to the point where
his relationship with his Lady begins to assume as much of a sado-
masochistic nature as social decorum permits. You might say he's
so in love that he's boorish, as for example when he suggests to
Donna Anna that they still get married the day after her father's
murder.

In truth, Ottavio is as narcissistic as everyone else in the
opera, less in love with Donna Anna as a person than he is in love
with the idea of being in love, or perhaps with the purely social
advantages of a good aristocratic match. It's a fantasy that he
will do anything to preserve. He remains utterly oblivious to the

notion that she might in fact be doing her best (nicely, of course) to suggest he turn his attentions elsewhere, and he is willing to do anything for her as long as he doesn't get his hands too dirty in the process. In his act 2 aria "Il mio tesoro" (No. 21), he revels in his lovesickness by asking the other characters to let Donna Anna know that he has gone to secure her peace of mind by alerting the proper authorities as to the identity of her father's murderer (rather than seeking revenge himself, as she clearly wants). The scoring for pairs of clarinets, bassoon, and horns, as previously mentioned, is not only consistent with the overall sonority of act 2, but embodies Mozart's preferred means of expressing the gentle sadness of unfulfilled love. The vocal line, with the big downward leap on the word "Vado," (the climax of the line "Tell her that I go to avenge the wrongs that she has suffered") and long-breathed phrasing, perfectly describes what might best be called Ottavio's aristocratic manliness. For all his good manners, he's not effete, and he's not a whiner.

For the Vienna version of the opera, Mozart replaced "Il mio tesoro" with act 1's "Dalla sua pace" (No. 10a). Because he's such a drip, some commentators have decried performing the opera in a manner that gives Don Ottavio two arias (neither of which is inordinately long), but there are better arguments in favor of including both of them. First, they are both incredibly beautiful arias; among the most ravishing ever written for the tenor voice. Second, he's an important character, whose participation can only further illuminate the fascinating personality of Donna Anna. Third, there's a certain Dostoyevskian realism in taking advantage of the opportunity to hear just how besotted Don Ottavio is, and this is entirely consistent with the Mozartean concept of character development through the music.

Finally, the two arias are not identical: "Il mio tesoro" is a request made of others; "Dalla sua pace" is an interior monologue and, as such, goes deeper into Don Ottavio's character (for better or worse). To see exactly how, turn to track 13 on the included CD. Here is the text of the aria:

Dalla sua pace la mia dipende;	My peace of mind depends on hers;
Quel che a lei piace vita mi rende,	Her pleasures give me life,
Quel che le incresce morte mi dà.	What saddens her brings me death.
S'ella sospira, sospiro anch'io;	If she sighs, I sigh too;
È mia quell'ira, quel pianto è mio;	Her anger is mine, her sorrow too;
E non ho bene, s'ella non l'ha.	And I cannot know joy if she has none.

First, we learn that Don Ottavio's life is totally in Donna Anna's hands, and as noted previously, the instrumental setting reflects this, being almost identical to her previous aria (the trumpets appear only in Donna Anna's recitative, not in the aria itself). But beyond that, pay particular attention to the music preceding the words "If she sighs, I sigh too." The little two-note motives are the standard symbolic musical representations of sighing and weeping, but the music isn't terribly sad at all (compare this to the same use of this motive in the Lachrymosa of the Requiem, CD track 17, where the sense of grief and suffering is overwhelming).

What Mozart is describing, in fact, is not just "sighing" in the generic sense but Donna Anna's sighs as Don Ottavio perceives them, through the rose-colored fog of true love. In other words, he loves everything about her, even her sadness and misery, and Mozart's sense of musical characterization is so acute and his technique so refined that he knows exactly how best to suggest this. This aria, then, offers a classic example of doing justice to the text while also deepening the audience's knowledge of the person singing it in a way that is entirely consistent with the dramatic context. This is why it would be unthinkable to cut this number for any reason other than pedantic notions of textural purity or the presence of a tenor who simply can't handle its considerable demands.

Donna Elvira

Donna Elvira's character is much simpler than Donna Anna's. She loves Don Giovanni, he left her, and she's been stalking him ever since trying to persuade him to change his ways and take her back. Some productions also suggest that she may be pregnant, but even with this added complication, her emotions and motivations remain clear. Indeed, one might say that because she's completely honest about what she truly wants and has no inhibitions in saying so, everyone else thinks she's out of her mind. She is, in fact, not nearly as crazy as Don Giovanni would like everyone else to believe, for she sees him as he really is, and her tormented state of mind results from the terrible knowledge that she's hopelessly in love with a complete degenerate.

Elvira sings three arias, two of which occur in act 1. The first, "Ah, chi mi dice mai" (No. 3), is scored for that special combination of clarinets, bassoons, and horns that Mozart turns to when he speaks of a yearning for love (here with a touch of anger mixed in). This aria actually turns into a trio, as Don Giovanni and Leporello comment on her desire to find her betrayer—and then to torture him to death and rip his heart out if he won't return to her. The music walks a fine line between feminine yearning and unbalanced fury, with both the vocal and instrumental parts full of wide leaps and jagged rhythms.

These slashing rhythms actually come to characterize Elvira's music, most graphically in her second aria, "Ah, fuggi" (No. 8), in which she beseeches Zerlina to run away from Don Giovanni and disregard his false promises. Scored for strings only, the aria's gaunt sonority and pervasively sharp rhythms have a distinctly baroque quality, the kind of thing more typical of opera seria, although with a length of about a minute, the music passes by too quickly to stop the action in the manner of a more fully developed "vengeance aria" from a bygone era. The very concision only enhances Elvira's force of personality.

Her third aria, the gorgeous "Mi tradì" (CD track 12) was added by Mozart for the Vienna performances, perhaps because Elvira's first aria is actually a trio (and dissolves into recitative, so there's no big ending to capture applause) and the second one is so short. Again Mozart justifies the inclusion of this extra number by revealing more about the character. In her first two arias, vengeance and despair dominate. Here, Elivra's love for Don Giovanni takes over:

Mi tradì quell'alma ingrata,	That ungrateful soul betrayed me,
Infelice, o Dio!, mi fa.	Unhappy he made me, O God!
Ma tradita e abbandonata,	But although betrayed and abandoned,
Provo ancor per lui pietà.	I still pity him.
Quando sento il mio tormento,	When I feel my anguish,
Di vendetta il cor favella;	My heart demands vengeance;
Ma, se guardo il suo cimento,	But when I see him in danger,
Palpitando il cor mi va.	My heart beats faster.

The scoring includes solo flute, clarinet, and bassoon, and when Elvira sings of love and pity, the vocal line rolls along in smooth, lyrical arches. But when she speaks of anguish and vengeance, the mood darkens and the jagged rhythms of her first two arias briefly return in the form of stabbing interjections from the woodwinds. Notice the perfect word setting of the last line: you can readily imagine Elvira's pounding heart. And unlike her first aria, this one has a big finish guaranteed to earn a storm of applause.

Leporello

Leporello is a *basso buffo,* or comic bass. As Don Giovanni's manservant and sidekick, he provides much of the opera's comic relief through irreverent and often cynical commentary on the behavior of everyone else. Mercenary, cowardly, craven, dishonest, and completely amoral, lacking even the gloss of gentlemanly behavior to which his boss pays lip service, one might say that he has no positive qualities that are not opportunistic. Still, Mozart gives him two arias. The second of these, "Ah, pieta" (No. 20), is an action number in which he talks himself out of a jam, and the scoring, with flutes the only treble woodwind, perfectly captures the shrill humor of the situation.

Leporello's first solo, popularly known as "The Catalogue Aria" (No. 4), offers a typically ambiguous combination of sympathy and cruelty. It's sympathetic because he is trying to persuade Donna Elvira of the futility of her pursuit, but at the same time cruel because he knows perfectly well just how angry the list of Don Giovanni's conquests will make her. This aria is also critical to the plot, because it is the only evidence of the title character's reputation and (theoretical) success as a lover, since over the course of the opera itself, everything Giovanni attempts ends in failure. This has given rise to a certain amount of speculation as to whether or not Leporello is simply making the whole thing up (the list is his idea, after all, and one can but wonder why he has kept it). You can listen on track 11 of the accompanying CD and judge for yourself. Note the sarcasm on the word "Ma," which begins the line "But in Spain, there are already a thousand and three."

Madamina, il catalogo è questo	My lady, here is the list
Delle belle che amo' il padron mio;	Of the beauties loved by my master;
Un catalogo egli è che ho fatt'io;	I made this list myself;
Osservate, leggete con me.	Observe. Read with me.

In Italia seicento e quaranta;	In Italy six hundred and forty;
In Almagna duecento e trentuna;	In Germany two hundred and thirty-one;
Cento in Francia, in Turchia novantuna;	One hundred in France, in Turkey ninety-one;
Ma in Ispagna son già mille e tre.	But in Spain there are already a thousand and three.
V'han fra queste contadine,	These include country girls,
Cameriere, cittadine,	Servants, townspeople,
V'han contesse, baronesse,	There are countesses, baronesses,
Marchesine, principesse.	Marquises, princesses.
E v'han donne d'ogni grado,	And women of every station,
D'ogni forma, d'ogni età.	Of every shape, of every season.
Nella bionda egli ha l'usanza	With the blondes he generally
Di lodar la gentilezza,	Praises their kindness,
Nella bruna la costanza,	With the brunettes their constancy,
Nella bianca la dolcezza.	With the fairest ones their sweetness.
Vuol d'inverno la grassotta,	He wants fat ones in winter,
Vuol d'estate la magrotta;	Thin ones in the summer;
È la grande maestosa,	The big ones are majestic,
La piccina e ognor vezzosa,	The little ones cute and dainty,
Delle vecchie fa conquista	He even goes after the elderly
Pel piacer di porle in lista;	For the pleasure of getting them on the list;
Sua passion predominante	His greatest passion
È la giovin principiante.	Is for the young beginners.
Non si picca-se sia ricca	He doesn't care if she's rich
Se sia brutta, se sia bella;	If she's ugly, if she's pretty;
Purché porti la gonella,	As long as she's wearing a skirt,
Voi sapete quel che fa.	You know what he does.

The comic manservant (almost invariably a bass or baritone) is a stock role, common to the genre of opera buffa. Mozart does not depart from this convention, but even when following tradition, there's an extra vividness and intelligence to the character that makes him come alive. Unlike so many of his type, Leporello is not stupid, and although no less degenerate than Don Giovanni, he gets through the opera with his skin intact. Given the fact that (at one point or another) all of the other characters, including Giovanni, threaten to murder him, that's no small testament to his survival skills.

Zerlina and Masetto

Masetto is the typical dumb peasant. He knows Don Giovanni is after his girl, but he's too stupid to do anything about it other than round up a gang to inflict some prairie justice, which badly backfires. His act 1 aria "Ho capito" (No. 6) offers the exact equivalent of Leporello's second aria (No. 20). It's scored exactly the same way and similarly expresses the frustration of a comic character in an uncomfortable situation. Zerlina, his girlfriend, is the music that soothes this particular beast. She's cute, perky, flirtatious, a little bit on the dim side too, flattered (at first) by Don Giovanni's attentions, and she almost becomes his victim at the end of act 1. She's the coy 50 percent of what is arguably the most famous flirtation duet in the entire operatic repertoire, "La ci darem la mano" (No. 7), or "Let's Hold Hands" (it sounds so much better in Italian). The tune is one of Mozart's greatest hits.

Zerlina would be another stock character were it not for the remarkable music that Mozart gives her. Her first aria, "Batti, batti" (No. 12), with its alarming text (Beat me, beat me, handsome Masetto) and remarkable solo cello part coiling around the vocal line like the bullwhip of some operatic dominatrix, comes across as a sort of classical-era predecessor to Tom Lehrer's "Masochism Tango." In her act 2 aria "Vedrai, carino" (No. 18), Zerlina looks over her beaten-up boyfriend and says to him: "Well, as long as the important parts are still working, come on home and I'll make you feel better." The aria, with its pairs of flutes, clarinets, bassoons, and horns, is remarkably sensual, even as the dancelike meter (3/8) reminds the audience that these are simple country folk, more open and frank about sexual matters than the opera's upper crust. Zerlina is, in fact, more complex than one might think; Masetto may seem too dumb for her, but she loves his devotion to her as well as her dominant role in their relationship.

Don Giovanni

I've saved the title character for last because, although he's the focus of everyone's attention, he has the least substantial music to sing. There's a very good reason for this. Arias reveal character, and Mozart and Da Ponte clearly don't want the audience to know anything about Don Giovanni. He is, above all, a mystery, expounded in three tiny arias. The first (No. 11), commonly called "The Champagne Aria," says nothing more than "Let's party and add a few more conquests in the process." His second aria, "Deh, vieni alla finestra" (No. 16), charmingly scored for pizzicato strings and mandolin, is a serenade under the balcony, requesting simply: "Come show your face honey, don't let me languish out here all alone," or words to that effect. The third aria, "Metà di voi" (No. 17), is an action piece in which Don Giovanni misleads Masetto's posse, and the text consists of little more than "You guys go this way, you others go that way, and grab any suspicious-looking couple that you see." The first two arias last less than two minutes each, the third less than three minutes. They are no more than teasers: brief flashes illuminating tiny portions of what is otherwise a huge, dark, and quite possibly empty room.

It's also worth noting, from a purely musical perspective, that none of Don Giovanni's solos feature clarinets. They appear as part of the full wind section in "The Champagne Aria" but aren't otherwise audible in the constantly full wash of sound, and one can take this as yet another sign that Mozart is unwilling to ascribe to him any profound emotions whatsoever. Indeed, Don Giovanni's character, to the extent that the audience learns anything about it at all, reveals itself much more fully in the duets and ensembles, where he shows himself to be at various times courageous, dashing, charming, callous, indifferent, insatiable, and even occasionally sympathetic in an offhand sort of way (he doesn't actually want to kill the Commendatore, for example, and does so only in self-defense).

What makes him such a mesmerizing figure, though, is the very aura of mystery that surrounds him, combined with the fact that he's drawn to his own demise like a moth to a flame. A person of such sphinxlike character demands a mythical end, which is exactly what Mozart and Da Ponte provide. Attempts by enthusiastic stage directors with a "concept" to explain his behavior almost invariably backfire. The less one knows of him the more impressive he becomes, the more real the other characters seem in contrast, and the stranger and more powerful the opera as a whole both looks and sounds.

The opera's final scene has caused a certain amount of controversy since the premiere. Da Ponte provided the work with a subtitle: *The Dissolute Man Punished,* and for many listeners this "moral" of the opera was its entire point. It is believed that Mozart himself cut the final scene at the Vienna premiere, and throughout the eighteenth century, the comic windup was considered shallow and offensive to Victorian standards of morality, and so the work usually ended with Don Giovanni's demise (which is not to say tragically, for he is certainly no tragic hero).

Whatever Mozart's ultimate intentions were in this respect, today it would be unthinkable to play the work without the final scene. I mentioned in the introduction to the opera that *Don*

Giovanni is a remarkably modern work, and this observation is nowhere truer than here. Its conclusion, in fact, plays like the end of a typical *Seinfeld* episode, in which the studied nonchalance of the characters and their relentless narcissism contrasts hilariously with their bizarre and even cruel behavior in the preceding scenes.

Here's the gist of the action: all the characters rush in looking for Don Giovanni. Leporello tells them he's just been relegated to eternal perdition. "So that's what happened," they all say, accepting his word with a little backing from Donna Elvira, who then tells everyone that she's decided to retire to a convent. Zerlina and Masetto go home to have supper together. Leporello is off to a tavern to find a better master. And as for Donna Anna and Don Ottavio, well, he asks, "Now can we finally get married?" She responds, "Let's wait another year darling. My heart needs to heal." Yeah, right. And off they go with a shrug, after uniting in a final chorus saying that those who misbehave always come to a bad end.

The question remains, however, just who has been behaving badly and to what end these characters will yet come. For ultimately Don Giovanni, considered in light of this final scene, has served as a sort of mirror, permitting them to see the ugly truth about themselves and each other, and in the end they refused to look. Their relief in his passing has, quite evidently, taught them nothing. At once funny, smart, and wickedly honest, this particular insight, cynical though it may be, crowns a work whose range of passion and incident, from its Hitchcock suspense-film opening to its *Seinfeld* sitcom ending, make it for many listeners the greatest opera ever written.

Così Fan Tutte
(They're All the Same)
1790

Introduction

Having celebrated the joys of psychological and emotional ambiguity in *Don Giovanni,* Mozart and Da Ponte decided to throw caution to the wind and write a work about little else. *Così fan tutte* is an opera that pretends to be about the faithfulness of women, but is really about seeing things as they truly are and people's capacity for self-deception. Now everyone knows that this last quality is practically limitless, but it's seldom comfortable to be reminded of the fact. And so the nineteenth and early twentieth centuries, sunk as they largely were in Victorian hypocrisy, loathed this opera as much as they loved *Don Giovanni* (without its final scene, of course). In its own day, when the Viennese theaters closed a month after the opera's premiere in January 1790 (owing to the death of the emperor and the ensuing official period of mourning), *Così* was on its way to being the most popular of the three Mozart/Da Ponte collaborations. Certainly it's the zaniest.

When I say that the plot and music are ambiguous, this does not mean uncertain, muddy, or in any way indistinct. Rather, it simply implies that the characters are richly multifaceted, that there is more than one way to interpret their actions, and that the work therefore repays repetition and always reveals something new at each encounter. In some respects, *Così* represents a simplification as compared with *Don Giovanni.* There are only six characters, three men and three women. All of them except Despina, the maid (who nonetheless plays a major role), come from the same class. The plot itself couldn't be sillier. Don Alfonso bets with his two young friends that he can prove the fickleness of their girlfriends within a day.

However, as with all good situation comedies, what matters is not the realism or plausibility of the scenario but rather the subtleties of its unfolding, the interaction between the characters, the comic timing of the various plot twists, and most importantly, how conscious (or more properly speaking, *unconscious*) the principals are of their own ridiculousness. If you already know *The Marriage of Figaro* or *Don Giovanni,* I'm sure you will see immediately that in this respect Mozart is on very firm ground, for he always supports his characters musically with total conviction and ensures that his audience believes what they believe and feels what they feel. Mozartean comedy is always serious, and that's what makes it enduringly funny as well as emotionally moving.

Moreover, the necessary willful suspension of disbelief becomes even easier because Mozart initially presents the young lovers in virtually identical terms: two besotted men making exaggerated claims about their women, followed by two equally besotted women making similarly excessive claims about their men. They actually complete each other's sentences with no break in thought or continuity, two mouths speaking with one voice. What follows over the next two acts is a gradual process of differentiation, especially noticeable in the frequently occurring duets (six of them, more than in any other major Mozart opera), in which these four scarcely credible stereotypes become four unique individuals.

So Mozart does not ask his audience to accept these cardboard cutouts as real people from the outset. Rather, he persuades his

	Così Fan Tutte: Quick Reference							
#	Title	Orchestration (in Addition to Strings)						
	Act 1	Flutes	Oboes	Clarinets	Bassoons	Horns	Trumpets	Timpani
1	Trio: La mia Dorabella capace non è		2		2	2		
2	Trio: È la fede delle femmine	1			1			
3	Trio: Una bella serenata		2		2		2	yes
4	Duet: Ah guarda sorella			2	2	2		
5	Aria: Vorrei dir			strings only				
6	Quintet: Sento, oddio, che questo piede			2	2	2		
7	Duet: Ah fato dan legge quegli occhi			2	2	2		
8	Chorus: Bella vita militar	2	2		2		2	yes
9	Quintet w/Chorus: Di scrivermi	2	2	2	2		2	yes
10	Terzettino: Soave sia il vento	2		2	2	2		
11	Aria: Smanie implacabile	2		2	2	2		
12	Aria: In uomini, in soldati	1	1		1			
13	Sextet: Alla bella Despinetta		2	2	2		2	yes
14	Aria: Come scoglio immota resta		2	2	2		2	
15	Aria: Non siate ritrosi	1			1			
	Aria: Rivolgete a lui lo squardo		2		2		2	yes
16	Trio: E voi ridete	2	2		2	2		
17	Aria: Un'aura amorosa			2	2	2		
18	Finale: Ah che tutta in un momento	2	2	2	2	2	2	yes
	Act 2							
19	Aria: Una donna a quindici anni	1			1	2		
20	Duet: Prenderò quel brunettino		2		2	2		
21	Duet w/Chorus: Secondate aurette	2		2	2	2	no strings	
22	Quartet: La mano a me date	2			2	2		
23	Duet: Il core vi dono, bell' idolo mio			2	2	2		
24	Aria: A lo veggio quell' anima bella			2	1		2	
25	Rondo: Per pietà, ben mio	2		2	2	2		
26	Aria: Donne mie la fate a tanti	2	2		2	2	2	yes
27	Cavatina: Tradito, schernito		2	2	2	2		
28	Aria: È amore un ladroncello	1	2	2	2	2		
29	Duet: Fra gli amplessi		2		2	2		
30	Andante: Tutti accusan le donne			strings only				
31	Finale: Fate presto o cari amici	2	2	2	2	2	2	yes

Table of Individual Numbers and Orchestration

listeners to do so by emphasizing, step by step, their gradually evident differences of opinion, their quirks of personality, and the truth of their emotional reactions. This method has the paradoxical result that, as with all great comedy, the sillier and more convoluted the situations become, the more believably (and true to their emerging selves) the characters behave.

The road to wisdom and self-knowledge in this particular case is paved with remarks that are sometimes shocking in their frankness, especially given our often rather courtly and bewigged image of Mozart and his era. When the two sisters ask themselves how they should spend their time while their boyfriends are off to battle, the following exchange ensues between Fiordiligi and the maid Despina:

> D: Why don't you think about how to amuse yourselves?
>
> F: (in transports of rage): Amuse ourselves?
>
> D: Sure. Even better, go and make love like assassins, exactly like your two sweethearts will be doing out there in the field.

Similarly, when Guglielmo (sometimes spelled Guilelmo) witnesses his beloved Fiordiligi's downfall at the hands of his disguised friend, Ferrando, his reaction couldn't be more graphic:

> So that's Fiordiligi! The Penelope, the Goddess of the century!
>
> Cheat, assassin, wretch, thief, bitch!

Even today you will sometimes find the words watered down to reflect more refined sensibilities. Now of course I'm not talking about anything X-rated (or even R-rated). What makes these exchanges telling is their honesty in the context of characters that spend most of the time claiming to recognize standards that are either false or hypocritical (or both). Indeed, there's nothing here as cruel or nasty as in *Don Giovanni*. The very first words of the opera's concluding ensemble might, in fact, stand as the official anthem of the Enlightenment:

> Happy is the man who makes the most of every situation,
> And through trials and misfortunes lets reason guide him.

Finally, of all Mozart's operas, *Così* is the one that has "modernized" the best. The comedy in *The Marriage of Figaro* arises from notions of social class that have no relevance today (even though the sexual-harassment premise that gets the story going is certainly adaptable enough). *Don Giovanni*'s recourse to the supernatural places it in the realm of fairy tale and legend, which is unquestionably the perspective from which its violence and moral ambivalence is most safely viewed. *Così fan tutte,* on the other hand, with its tight focus on the interaction among four characters of equal standing manipulated by two "outsiders," has shown itself infinitely adaptable, working as well in modern dress as in period costume. It depends for its success neither on local color nor on artificial or absurd conventions nor on the customs of a specific social milieu, but rather on the fact that in the two centuries since it was written, it's not just the girls who continue to behave similarly. We all do.

Music and Characters *

Overture

The chapter "Mozart's Operatic Style" discusses the relationship between the deliciously gossipy overture and the opening scene, but there's a lot more that's noteworthy about these four

---

* Keep in mind that the initial two pairs of lovers at the beginning of the opera are Ferrando/Dorabella and Guglielmo/Fiordiligi. The two men return in disguise after wagering with Don Alfonso on the faithfulness of the two women, and each then attempts to seduce the other's girlfriend.

minutes of fun. First, the slow introduction ends with a musical recitation of the opera's title (CD track 2 at 0:18 and later, just before the end, at 3:28): "Co-sì-fan-tuuuuuuuuut-te," exactly as Don Alfonso and his male friends will sing it in act 2. Mozart does not expect that you will remember this motive, and you certainly don't need to for any special reason other than the pleasure of knowing that it's there.

The ensuing allegro, however, does reveal something about what makes this particular opera special. It has three main components: a string crescendo (at 0:31) leading to a sort of "Hallelujah Chorus" on the trumpets and drums (at 0:39), a wispy bit of syncopated hand-wringing for the strings in a minor key (at 1:07), and in between them a chattering sequence of eight-note arabesques tossed back and forth by the woodwinds in every conceivable order and combination (at 0:43). Mozart then shuffles these ideas around like a pack of cards. If you look at the orchestration chart and compare it to those of *The Marriage of Figaro* and *Don Giovanni,* you will see clearly that Mozart's scoring has become steadily more dense in the woodwind department, and it reaches a sort of apotheosis here, most obviously in "Secondate aurette" (No. 21), a duet with chorus that is scored for voices and wind octet only, with no strings at all.

Great wind playing was very much a Central European specialty based primarily in Bohemia (the tradition is still alive today). Many of the best players resident in Vienna and working in the great aristocratic houses (and of course in Prague) came from this school, and Mozart knew them well. His writing for woodwind instruments of all kinds was considered extremely difficult, even excessive. Some critics complained that it stole attention away from the singers and covered the voices. It rendered his operas virtually unperformable in other countries (Italy especially), and although you will not find in *Così* any additional instruments such as piccolo, basset horns, Turkish percussion, and trombones, or any special effects such as a serenading mandolin or onstage bands, the amount of color that Mozart produces with what seems today to be a very modest compliment of instruments is astonishing.

As in the previous two works, there is the consistent use of pairs of clarinets, bassoons, and horns (sometimes with flutes) in arias and ensembles expressing longing for love or sadness and despair at its loss or absence. Given the fact that this idea permeates the entire opera whether or not the characters are faking it (sometimes they are and sometimes they aren't), the result is that in act 1 alone this characteristically Mozartean sonority is found in Nos. 4, 6, 7, 10, 11, and 17. In practical terms, this means that the clarinets (playing in seventeen numbers in total) have at last reached a level of absolute equality with the oboes (sixteen numbers). No other composer of the period wrote for the then newly improved clarinet with such enthusiasm and understanding of its special expressive character.

Even more remarkably, Mozart now treats trumpets, both with and without timpani, very freely. The use of the brighter-toned trumpets in preference to the horns and without the usual accompaniment of drums, as in Nos. 14, 22, and 24, gives the scoring a luminous quality and rhythmic clarity new not just to Mozart but to the classical orchestra in general. As you listen, you will discover that having more instruments available to play in each number casts a subtly varied and ravishing wash of color over the entire score, offering nearly infinite opportunities to blend timbres and inflect the melodic lines. And Mozart offers the perfect preview in this sunny, comical, loquacious little overture.

Don Alfonso and Despina

These two characters belong together because they form a team as the opera proceeds, although their motives are quite different. All the audience knows about Don Alfonso is that he's older, cynical, and enters into the wager that he can turn the heads of the two women out of (he would have his two friends believe) benevolence. He maintains that true happiness is impossible without a firm grip on reality. Beyond that, Mozart says nothing about him, and it is very significant that he has but one aria in the entire opera, "Vorrei dir" (No. 5), accompanied by strings only and lasting about half a minute. The text is basically "I have big news but I don't know how to break it to you," and the monochrome orchestral coloring makes the music as neutrally flavored as the character singing it. Beyond that, Don Alfonso is less a person than a mechanism that moves the plot along.

Despina, on other hand, is very much an individual, and living proof that even in Mozart's day, good help was hard to come by. She is the maid from hell, smarter than her two charges, sharp-tongued, mercenary, disloyal, coarse, and either very funny or very annoying, depending on your perspective and on how well the singer knows how to act with her voice. As the icon of hedonistic cynicism, love has no place in her philosophy, and so accordingly you will find no clarinets in either of her arias. She's strictly a flute, oboe, and bassoon kind of gal, but she's important for a couple of reasons. First, she reminds the audience in her first aria, "In uomini, in soldati" (No. 12), that the opera's subtitle, *The School for Lovers,* applies to both pairs equally. She points out in words that brook no dispute that the very idea of faithfulness is a double standard imposed on women by men who wouldn't understand the term if their lives depended on it.

Her second aria, "Una donna a quindici anni" (No. 19), goes even further: by the age of fifteen, a woman should be experienced in the ways of the world and capable of manipulating men to her advantage. She believes her message is getting through to the two ladies, but in the end the joke is at least partly on her. Because she only understands and delights in deception, she remains oblivious to Don Alfonso's larger purpose (as it transpires) of proving that true love exists only in acceptance of the other's shortcomings. So when the pairs of lovers are reunited at the end, having essentially accepted in some measure Despina's premises and arrived at very different conclusions as a result, she is shocked and disappointed. Again, depending on whether you view her as amusingly simple or simply obnoxious, her isolation from the others can appear either touchingly sad or exactly what she deserves. Perhaps it's both. Although usually played mostly for laughs, there's more to Despina than just her smart-alecky surface.

Fiordiligi

Guglielmo's girlfriend is an extremely rich, complex, and sympathetic character, and she gets two of Mozart's very best arias. Less emotionally unstable than her sister and far more serious of mind, Mozart captures her personality perfectly in the first of them, "Come scoglio" ("Like a Rock"—No. 14), the words to which express her conviction that she is immovably faithful unto death. Mozart's orchestration is particularly brilliant here. Essentially this is a military number, full of aptly heroic gestures from the trumpets that are echoed by the voice, but significantly, the accompaniment omits the timpani. This permits Fiordiligi to express firmness without excessive machismo, in an aptly feminine sort of way. It also suggests that the fortress of her determination may be lacking a little something in the way of a firm foundation.

Reinforcing this last idea is the opening vocal line, with leaps from the top to the bottom of the voice so wide as to be comical. This sort of gesture, a huge and sudden change of register at full strength, is actually a cliché of opera seria, where arias expressing heroic determination and faithfulness under pressure are legion. But there's one big difference: there, the issue is usually a horrible death or some other form of physical or mental torture, and not the threat of a blind date with an exotic stranger. So the circumstances hardly warrant a full-blown opera seria–style reply, and the whole thing is wonderfully exaggerated. In retrospect, those huge intervals at the opening in which Fiordiligi believes that she is expressing resolve turn out to be emotional chasms wide enough to drive a truck (or a guy disguised as an Albanian) through. You can hear this seriocomic masterpiece on the accompanying CD, track 14.

Come scoglio immoto resta	Like a rock, standing fast
Contra i venti, e la tempesta,	Against wind and storm,
Così ognor quest'alma è forte	This soul stands strong
Nella fede, e nell'amor.	In faithfulness and love.
Con noi nacque quella face	Within us the flame is born
Che ci piace, e ci consola,	That grants delight and comfort,
E potrà la morte sola	And only death itself
Far che cangi affetto il cor.	Can alter the dictates of the heart.
Rispettate, anime ingrate,	Respect, you miserable wretches,
Questo esempio di constanza,	This example of constancy,
E una barbara speranza	Never permit your barbaric hopes
Non vi renda audaci ancor.	To again make you audacious.

Note the juicy text. This is the language of opera seria, high-toned and loaded with pompous (and rather meaningless) symbolism about things like fidelity and virtue. The last stanza is particularly marvelous in its positively epic expression of contempt for the two disguised suitors. An operatic soprano who can't make a meal of this number, rearing up like a wrathful

Greek goddess and heaping scorn on all and sundry, really needs to look for a new job. Yes, the aria is only half serious, but it should be sung perfectly straight, and the fact that Fiordiligi may be protesting too much (in a great performance at least) will only strike you *after* she storms off stage, leaving the others (and the audience) suitably impressed.

To compare "Come scoglio" to Fiordiligi's act 2 aria, "Per pieta" (No. 25), is to enjoy an object lesson in how Mozart develops character through music. All of the elements of Fiordiligi's first aria are here: the wide range (two full octaves from low to high B) defined by huge vocal leaps, and the jagged rhythms. But now the situation is very different. She feels herself attracted to the disguised Ferrando, and she hates herself for it. The trumpets and oboes are gone, replaced by the flutes and clarinets that express sadness in Mozartean musical language. A rondo is simply an aria in two tempos, first slow, then fast (Donna Anna's "Non mi dir" in *Don Giovanni* is another example). The opening slow section makes a point of those big jumps from the bottom of the voice to the top, only instead of appearing confident, Fiordiligi sounds exhausted, weighted down by despair, almost moaning. The wind solos separating her broken phrases only add to the feeling of loneliness.

In the quick section, as she regains her resolve and swears to remain faithful to Guglielmo, a remarkable thing happens. As in Donna Anna's rondo, there's plenty of vocal flash in the form of coloratura, but whereas Anna's music sounds strangely at odds with the words, suggesting that she has something quite different on her mind, Fiordiligi's music is darker and more subdued, more rooted in the text. Specifically, Mozart makes the vocal virtuosity clearly symbolic of Fiordiligi's returning confidence. The ornamentation, and in particular that last spectacular two-octave stretch, progressively fills in the gaps between those wide intervals and gives Fiordiligi's newfound conviction a genuine musical foundation that reinforces the meaning of the words and gives them substance.

This in turn will render her final, equivocal surrender to the disguised Ferrando a truly poignant moment. From then until the end of the opera, Fiordiligi remains morally tormented by the knowledge of her own weakness. By the same token, the eventual happy ending (if that's what it is) becomes a resolution we actively want to see because we care about this character and her ultimate fate. There's more to the evolution of Fiordiligi's character than these two arias, and this will be discussed shortly, but what makes comparison of them so fascinating is hearing how Mozart the musical portrait painter turns what was, in act 1, an impressive line drawing into a naturalistic oil on canvas.

Dorabella

In the trio that opens the opera, Ferrando and Guglielmo describe their respective girlfriends with identical music, but already in their two first arias, even though they express the same sentiments, Mozart reveals how wrong this initial picture of them actually is. Dorabella, a bit of a ditz, has nothing like Fiordiligi's heroic grandeur of character and sheer hauteur. Both of her arias are short in duration and quick in tempo, revealing her shallowness of temperament and lack of emotional depth. The first of them, "Smanie implacabile" (No. 11), lasts less than two minutes and basically says, "I would rather die than endure the torment of my boyfriend's absence." And this comes after one of the funniest (because so excessively tragic) recitatives in the entire opera. "Close the windows," she orders Despina, "I hate the light!"

Whirling triplets in the strings describe her physical agitation, while the steady repetition of lines of the very short text illustrates her equally strongly revolving thoughts. Only at the end does the music pause briefly, so that the woodwinds can emit a brief sigh of despair as she describes her own sighs at the wretchedness of tragic love. The quiet ending reveals this particular storm, however, to have little sustaining force. Note that Fiordiligi's aria is a reaction against the first attempts at seduction by the disguised suitors, and speaks of her high moral principals. Dorabella, on the other hand, has nothing to say about her resolve to remain faithful, as she has not yet met the "Albanians." She's just upset and venting her distress.

Her second aria, "E amore un ladroncello" (No. 28), says that "love is a little thief," a viper that sinks its fangs into your heart and then forces you to follow wherever it leads. Like that of her sister, Dorabella's character has altered, but in the opposite direction. Mozart accordingly changes her music to reflect its emotional distance from Fiordiligi's. In the latter's second aria, "Per pietà," Mozart takes the basic style of vocal expression and gives it new emotional depth and meaning by developing and transforming Fiordiligi's personal musical gestures. He does something quite different with Dorabella. She has decided to have a little fun with disguised Guglielmo and is urging Fiordiligi to join her. Indeed, she has become Despina's protégé.

"E amore un ladroncello" begins with a refrain for flute, clarinets, bassoons, and horns alone—in other words, with Mozart's most plangent love music—exactly as in the duet-with-chorus "Secondate aurette" (No. 21), in which the two men poetically beg that their protestations of love be favorably answered. Once Dorabella actually begins singing, however, strings join in as well as the two oboes, and this, combined with the 6/8 "pastoral" time signature, places the aria squarely in the world of Despina's previous aria, No. 19. So instead of developing Dorabella's music as he did Fiordiligi's, Mozart instead fuses the love music of No. 21 with the rhythm, tempo, and timbre of her maid's special brand of expression, and demonstrates in this way that Dorabella has now gone over entirely to the other side.

This may sound complicated, but it really isn't. Fiordiligi's music highlights her consistency, while Dorabella's illustrates her fickleness. What makes Mozart's practice so fascinating is not how diabolically clever it looks on paper to music theorists but rather how logical, practical, and totally grounded in the basic facts of the drama his musical characterizations are and, accordingly, how well they actually work in the theater. No one, least of all Mozart, expects you to say, "Aha! Aria No. 28 is basically a conflation, albeit with different tunes, of Nos. 19 and 21!" All that really matters is that when Dorabella expresses her newfound determination to live it up, you believe in the genuineness of her conversion because musically it arises organically from what has come before. Mozart's treatment of the two sisters not only represents the very essence of the great opera composer, but it also shows how much he cares about making what is happening on stage clear to his listeners in the most direct manner possible. His method isn't so much complicated as it is breathtakingly efficient and, above all, accurate.

Guglielmo

Like Dorabella, Guglielmo is a shallow character, not given to reflection. He believes in Fiordiligi's fidelity not so much because he trusts her as because he can't imagine why any woman would look at another man when she can have him. This, Mozart proceeds to illustrate, is not exactly the best foundation on which to build a relationship. Fiordiligi in fact takes Guglielmo much more seriously than he takes her. His first aria, "Non siate ritrosi" (No. 15), is a breezy andante that basically says to the ladies (and this after the great exordium of "Come scoglio"), "Come on over and check out us two prime hunks of male beefcake." The music is amusingly trivial, the text hilariously graphic as to the specifics (the disguised men's fake mustaches are "love's plumage"). The entire aria, like Dorabella's first number, lasts less than two minutes. Its scoring includes only strings plus one flute and one bassoon: Guglielmo, like Despina, never sings of love or expresses sadness in his arias. Neither of them features clarinets.

His second aria, "Donne mie" (No. 26) in act 2, is another comic number that purports to sympathize with Ferrando, whose girlfriend Dorabella has just caved in to Guglielmo's efforts at seduction. The bustling accompaniment and heavy scoring with trumpets and drums offers an intensification of the theme of the first aria: it's a wonder that men put up with women, cute and cuddly as they are, when they are always cheating and deceiving their better halves. It is in fact the male counterpart of Despina's first aria. The breezy arrogance of this piece perfectly sets up Guglielmo for the big fall when Fiordiligi ultimately capitulates to Ferrando.

Indeed, hypocrite that he is, he takes Fiordiligi's downfall much, much harder than Ferrando does Dorabella's because of the insult it represents to his pride. In the fake wedding scene in the act 2 finale, when all of the other characters are getting into the spirit of the occasion (or pretending to) and making a toast, Guglielmo alone stands aside and mutters, "Their drinks should be poisoned, those shameless tramps," and Mozart's music deftly singles him out and separates him from the ensemble. Indeed it remains an open question just how reconciled he really is with the opera's supposed happy ending.

Finally, Guglielmo's character requires one bit of musical housekeeping: the aria "Rivolgete a lui" (No. 15a) was replaced in the original production by "Non siate ritrosi" (No. 15). Many recordings include 15a as an appendix, but it is seldom performed on stage. Although differently scored than No. 15, note that it also includes neither clarinets nor even the full compliment of Guglielmo's second-act aria, and so offers additional evidence of Mozart's ultimate intentions with respect to the musical treatment of the role. The text says essentially the same thing in both cases, but in 15a it takes twice as long to say it, hence the generally perceived superiority of its shorter replacement.

Ferrando

Ferrando is a genuinely nice guy, and a true romantic tenor of a type rarely found in opera until later in the nineteenth century. In Mozart's previous two Italian operas, the most important male roles went not to tenors but to baritones (Figaro, the Count, Don Giovanni, and Leporello). Guglielmo is also a baritone. If Mozart illustrates Guglielmo's comparatively superficial character by a process of absorption, adding a layer of Despina-like cynicism (similar to Dorabella's) to his natural arrogance, then you might call the process Ferrando undergoes one of variation (similar to Fiordiligi's). Just as none of Guglielmo's solos has clarinets, every one of Ferrando's includes them (and he has three, more than anyone else). His act 1 aria, "Un'aura amorosa" (No. 17), is a straightforward hymn to love, and to the two sisters. Note that Mozart only gradually introduces the woodwinds, increasing the music's sense of yearning with each repetition of the words.

Ferrando's second aria, "Ah, lo veggio" (No. 24 in act 2), represents his attempted seduction of Fiordiligi, but Mozart has replaced the mellow horns with the more cutting trumpets, whose timbre really begins to tell toward the end of the piece when Ferrando says that he will die if she leaves him. The variation in timbre is subtle—particularly as the dynamics are mostly quiet, and once again Mozart adds the winds gradually, creating a steady intensification of color and emotion—but the trumpets do help project Ferrando's affected passion in more extroverted terms than in "Un'aura amorosa," which is an interior monologue rather than a plea addressed to Fiordiligi.

Finally we come to Mozart's third and most wonderful variation on the love theme, "Tradito, schernito" (No. 27). To the basic wind ensemble of clarinets, bassoons, and horns, there is an unlikely visitor: a pair of oboes. Here's what in fact happens. Ferrando proclaims the opening line, "Betrayed, scorned, by a treacherous heart," to jagged rhythms. Then follows a little refrain for clarinets and bassoons, introducing the words "I feel my soul still adores her, and I feel for her what the voices of love tell me." That is the entire text of the aria. After singing it through, the singer begins again, exactly as before, with the opening line. Only this time, the oboes replace the clarinets in the refrain and continue to accompany the voice plaintively. The meaning is clear: the fine wine of Ferrando's love has turned to vinegar. However as his thoughts dwell once again on the "voices of love" and the vocal line expands into the aria's conclusion, the clarinets join the oboes, and together they bring the piece to its quiet close, perfectly illustrating Ferrando's ambivalence.

In concluding this discussion of the lovers, it's worthwhile to summarize the points touched on so far. All four begin essentially on the same page: with the notion that their significant other is perfection incarnate. From this false premise, their characters begin to diverge, and Mozart illustrates this process by creating musical analogues to their actions and words. Fiordiligi and Ferrando both deepen and develop from within, as Mozart subjects their music to an evolutionary process of variation. But the important point is that the *kind* of music that describes them (the wide vocal leaps of Fiordiligi, the romantic clarinets of Ferrando) remains consistent throughout. Dorabella and Gulglielmo, on the other hand, change in response to external influence: they progressively adopt Despina's cynical philosophy, allowing her characteristic music to infiltrate and increasingly define their personalities. By this process, Mozart's writing for them suggests that they lack the firmness of spirit that defines Fiordiligi and Ferrando, and as you will see shortly, this also throws into question both the wisdom of the original pairings at the opera's outset and the exact nature of the "happy" ending.

The Duets

As mentioned previously, *Così fan tutte* is also very much an opera of ensembles, of interaction between these increasingly complex and continually evolving individuals. So I'll wrap up with a very brief survey of the six duets. This will illustrate even more clearly just how consistently Mozart applies the musical language that he has created for his characters.

No. 4: The two sisters are singing rapturously about their two gentlemen as they stare, love struck, at their portraits. The scoring is classic Mozartean love music: pairs of clarinets, bassoons, and horns with strings.

No. 7: Exactly the same scoring for exactly the same sentiment: the two men take their leave, promising that love will guide them back swiftly to the welcoming arms of their respective beloveds.

No. 20: Led by Dorabella, the two sisters decide how to divide up the two phony Albanians. The tone color and musical language, with oboes prominent, belong to Despina.

No. 21: As discussed previously, this is the beautiful scene accompanied by wind octet, in which the two men ask the breezes to carry the message of their love to the sisters. The scoring is "pure" love music, with no strings, and two flutes suggesting the soft breezes mentioned in the text.

No. 23: Guglielmo seduces Dorabella, and he does it (orchestrally at least) by sounding like Ferrando:

it's the same scoring as the first two duets and, more significantly, "Un'aura amorosa."

No. 29: Ferrando seduces Fiordiligi and does so in the musical language of Guglielmo (meaning no clarinets). The actual circumstances further reinforce Mozart's decision to withhold the characteristic timbres of his love music. Fiordiligi capitulates more out of pity, exasperation, and exhaustion than enthusiasm, and Ferrando only persuades her by threatening suicide. He's desperate, and she's miserable.

Finally, it's worth noting two further points. First, by the time the women ultimately capitulate, the audience never really knows exactly what they believe that they are agreeing to. Dorabella speaks of belonging to another and just having a little fun, while Fiordiligi certainly isn't happy with her situation, remaining doubtful and guilt-ridden. So is the ensuing (fake) wedding all part of the same game or something that they actually seriously want to happen? Personally, I don't think that they are fooled for long. There's evidence to support both arguments: Mozart and Da Ponte wisely leave the matter open to question. The same sort of ambiguity occurs at the end of Shakespeare's *The Taming of the Shrew*. Has Kate's will really been broken, or has she just learned to carry on her rebellion more diplomatically?

Second, some productions make a point of rearranging the couples at the end, because as the story progresses, it begins to look increasingly as though they were mismatched at the opera's start. Just as one must consider the possibility that the women are faking it as much as the men, it's also entirely possible that the effort of seduction has caused at least one of the men (Ferrando) to fall in love with Guglielmo's girl, and for Guglielmo to hate everyone involved. Additionally, the audience has learned that the two most serious characters and kindred spirits are Ferrando and Fiordiligi, while Dorabella and Guglielmo are both shallower (and certainly more comic).

Most significantly, Mozart's musical characterizations strongly suggest that this might in fact be the way the couples finally end up (unless one takes the position that opposites invariably attract). So the opera's ending is one of those cases where judging what it all means and determining the believability of the final resolution is part of the fun. Certainly it provides an excellent reason to see the piece in new productions on multiple occasions, and it drives home once again the fact that Mozart provides only as many notes as are necessary. Too much information can be as dramatically deadening as too little, and knowing what not to reveal is just as valuable a dramatic gift.

Still, *Così fan tutte* remains a long opera. It usually plays for about three hours when given uncut, and the reason for this is the same as the reason that "Marten aller Arten" is the biggest aria in *The Abduction from the Seraglio*: expressing character through music takes time, and creating four believable and interesting characters (five including Despina) therefore inevitably demands a long-term commitment. But in the end, most listeners agree that it's time well spent. The subject of *Così* is trivial only to those who believe that the search for true love and happiness is trivial, and the action is sometimes silly because real people often behave foolishly, deluding both themselves and others—even with the best will in the world. Although *Così* isn't as obviously funny as *Figaro* or as physically exciting as *Don Giovanni*, it remains without question the most purely sensual of all Mozart's theatrical works, the most gorgeously written, as well as the most human. And that's saying a lot.

La Clemenza di Tito
(The Mercy of Titus)
1791

Introduction

This is the "comeback kid" among Mozart's mature operas. Popular in the years immediately after its premiere at the coronation festivities in Prague for Leopold II, it sank into near total oblivion for more than a century and a half, gradually gaining favor only in the last few decades of the twentieth century. Several factors account for its disappearance. The first and most entertaining, if least important, is the possibly apocryphal fact that Leopold's new bride loathed the work, referring to it as *una porcheria tedesca,* or "German trash." Coming from an Italian aristocrat of the day, especially on the subject of Mozart, "German" in this context might very well have meant *too much music,* an excessive focus on instrumental richness of texture, and not enough sheer vocal razzle-dazzle. Anyway, it hardly matters, and posterity has had its revenge, since her theoretically great-and-serene highness is remembered today solely for her stupidity in dismissing Mozart's *La clemenza di Tito.*

The second factor getting in the way of modern performances was the convention in opera seria of giving the lead male role to a castrato. By 1791 this creepy and disgusting vocal classification was well on its way out, but the necessity in modern performances of using grown women in adult male roles (as opposed to the so-called trouser roles such as the young page Cherubino in *Figaro*) mitigated against the acceptance of all works in this genre (as if people singing at each other for hours on end is otherwise perfectly normal). This in turn leads to the third and most important factor in the opera's slow acceptance: the fact that it is an opera seria in the first place.

Even more than in *Idomeneo,* the structure and format of *Tito* follow age-old conventions. The libretto, by that Shakespeare of opera seria Pietro Metastasio, was written in the 1730s and set by an endless series of composers that no one cares about today, dozens upon dozens of times. Unlike comic opera, so-called serious opera (which need not end tragically, by the way, only more or less logically) is not about regular folks looking for love. It describes larger-than-life characters and the conflict between desires of the heart and the eternal principals of justice, duty, honor, sacrifice, friendship, mercy, and heroism. This makes the genre an ideal vehicle for state occasions intended to praise the new monarch, or wish him well at some special commemoration by describing the idyllic lives of the happy populace under his invariably enlightened and benevolent rule.

Inevitably, this means that anyone looking for a high level of romantic passion in *Tito,* or just about any other opera seria, is likely to be disappointed. The dramatic structure of such works does not support the kind of evolving, dynamic growth of character found in Mozart's previous three operas. Personalities don't change: they get themselves into sticky situations and then express emotions accordingly, generally one per aria. This makes a certain logical sense when you consider the fact that it's not a good idea from a public-policy perspective to present the ruler of a great empire as someone who has a lot to learn, lacks constancy and maturity, or otherwise starts emotionally at point A and winds up at the end of the opera at point B, exhibiting laughable

#	Title	Flutes	Oboes	Clarinets	Bassoons	Horns	Trumpets	Timpani
	La Clemenza di Tito: Quick Reference							
	Orchestration (in Addition to Strings)							
	Act 1							
1	Duet: Come ti piace, imponi	1	2		2	2		
2	Aria: Deh se piacer mi vuoi	2			2	2		
3	Duettino: Deh prendi un dolce amplesso			2	2	2		
4	March	2	2	2	2	2	2	yes
5	Chorus: Serbate, o Dei custodi	2		2	2	2		
6	Aria: Del più sublime soglio	2			2	2		
7	Duet: Ah perdona al primo affetto	1	2		2			
8	Aria: Ah, se fosse intorno		2		2	2		
9	Aria: Parto, parto		2	1 solo	2	2		
10	Trio: Vengo! Aspettate!	2	2		2	2		
11	Recitative: Oh Dei, che smania e questa		2		2	2		
12	Finale: Deh conservate	2	2	2	2	2	2	yes
	Act 2							
13	Aria: Torna di Tito a lato			strings only				
14	Trio: Se a volto mai ti senti		2		2	2		
15	Chorus: Ah grazie si rendano	2		2	2	2		
16	Aria: Tardi s'avvede		2			2		
17	Aria: Tu fosti tradito		2		2	2		
18	Trio: Quello di Tito è il volto	2		2	2	2		
19	Rondo: Deh, per questo istante	1	2		2	2		
20	Aria: Se all'impero, amici Dei	2	2		2	2		
21	Aria: S'altro che lagrime	1	1		1	2		
22	Recitative: Ecco il punto			strings only				
23	Rondo: Non più di fiori	1	2	1 basset horn	2	2		
24	Chorus: Che del ciel	2	2		2	2	2	yes
25	Recitative: Ma, che giorno			strings only				
26	Finale: Tu, è ver, m'assolvi	2	2	2	2	2	2	yes

Table of Individual Numbers and Orchestration

if normal human foibles in between. Politicians of all eras tend to take themselves seriously.

On the other hand, as long as the obligatory fawning and praise don't become too obsequious, there is absolutely no reason why the emotions depicted in opera seria need be any less intense, varied, or true merely because they are organized and presented differently than in the kinds of opera that supplanted it in the public favor in later generations. Quite the opposite, in fact. Opera seria offers an ideal vehicle for the expression of emotion in music across a broad range of character types. Mozart loved it for just this reason. As discussed, it is exactly this serious element that accounts for the depth of feeling on display in his comedies.

The revival of baroque opera over the past several decades, along with the recovery of period performance practices of both playing and singing, has demonstrated conclusively that these works can in fact make terrific theater, and that within their own genre, they offer as much variety and contrast as most other musical art forms. Accepting their conventions has proven no more difficult for today's audiences than dealing with the fundamental suspension of disbelief required by any other type of opera. The result of this healthy trend was that by the 1970s or so, the time was right for a reappraisal of opera seria in general and *Tito* in particular.

So instead of wondering why Mozart wrote the piece at all (he did it for the money, as with everything else he composed save perhaps the six quartets dedicated to Haydn), consider instead how Mozart took this theoretically dated form and turned it into something inimitably Mozartean. Far from coming across as faded and uninteresting, *Tito* in fact contains at least three of his very greatest individual arias, and a rich assortment of other beautiful numbers, including some marvelous ensembles and choruses.

Indeed, the choruses actually give an excellent clue as to what makes Mozart's vision of an opera seria special. They feature prominently in *Idomeneo,* for example, but have no place in Metastasio's original libretto for *Tito.* Mozart and his librettist, Caterino Mazzolà (to whom he gave the credit for turning the time-worn text into a "true opera") added them as part of a wholesale modernizing process that also involved reducing the original three acts to the by-now-customary two. These choruses are extremely important for several reasons. First, as in *Idomeneo,* they enlarge the opera's frame of reference, introducing a new character in the form of "the people," and in so doing they allow for a musical contrast between the private interactions of the characters and the larger political context that frames the story.

You can hear this most graphically in the finale to act 1, where the individual reflections of the characters to the torching of the capitol serve as the foreground, with the anguished cries of the chorus in the background. *Tito* lacks the sort of action-music ensembles found in the comic operas, and in particular it forgoes lengthy finales in exchange for more stately tableaux in which everyone freezes and expresses a single overriding emotion. That said, the action builds no less surely to these imposing conclusions than in any other dramatic work of Mozart's (and in stark contrast to *Idomeneo*). In act 1, the sequence of Nos. 10–12 (the recitatives included in the orchestration chart are all accompanied) creates twelve or thirteen minutes of continuous music. In act 2, the last thirty minutes or so of the opera contain only about four or five minutes' worth of simple recitative. Indeed, the greatest aria in the entire opera, Vitellia's "Non più di fiori," runs directly into the succeeding march and chorus, and so initiates the grand closing scene of reconciliation.

Mozart also characterizes the chorus very interestingly, as a collective personality. I already discussed how the characteristic wind ensemble of clarinets, bassoons, and horns (often with flutes) frequently characterizes feelings of love, tenderness, or yearning. Titus's people love him. Accordingly, have a look at the scoring of "Ah grazie" (No. 15). It's as moving a love song as Mozart ever wrote, and it includes a very effective solo for Titus himself that reveals, in effect, that the only love he truly feels is for his people. Even though he inevitably comes across as saintly to the point of disbelief, Mozart at least gives the audience an opportunity to understand him from a more human perspective.

Leaving aside this second-act chorus, there are two more extremely important and interesting places in this opera where Mozart's most affectionate musical symbolism is found. The first of these is the tiny duet in act 1, "Deh prendi" (No. 3), in which Annius and Sextus proclaim their undying friendship to one another. Even more fascinating is the trio in act 2, "Quello di Tito" (No. 18), in which Titus confronts the traitor and would-be murderer Sextus, whom he once thought a friend. The key to the music can be found in the words of Publius: "A thousand different emotions are at war within Titus. If he feels that much conflict, surely he yet loves Sextus." Mozart's music seconds this thought, and it also reveals that this particular scoring colors not only feelings of romantic, physical love but tenderness and affection of every kind. The musical language adapts to different circumstances while keeping its fundamentals intact.

With four major exceptions (that I will consider below at the appropriate time), all of the arias and ensembles in this opera are quite short. Indeed, this is the briefest of all of Mozart's late operas by a good margin, playing for just a bit over two hours on average, one hour for each act. Its elegant proportions point to the significance of Mozart's achievement, for if he slowed down the language of comedy to provide for richer characterizations

Le Nozze di Figaro

Renée Fleming as the Countess and Susanne Mentzer as Cherubino.

The Countess
Act II

Costume sketches by
James Acheson.

Rebecca Evans as Susanna, Hei-Kyung Hong as the Countess, Susan Graham as Cherubino.

Dwayne Croft as the Count and Hei-Kyung Hong as the Countess.

Michel Sénéchal as Don Basilio, Korliss Uecker as Susanna, Peter Mattei as Count Almaviva. Costume sketches by James Acheson.

Così Fan Tutte

Carol Vaness as Fiordiligi, Jerry Hadley as Ferrando, Thomas Allen as Don Alfonso, Cecilia Bartoli as Despina, Dwayne Croft as Guglielmo, Susanne Mentzer as Dorabella.

Rodney Gilfry as Guglielmo,
Dawn Upshaw as Despina,
Paul Groves as Ferrando.

Dwayne Croft as Guglielmo,
Carol Vaness as Fiordiligi.

Renée Fleming as Fiordiligi.

Don Giovanni

Ferruccio Furlanetto as Leporello,
Bryn Terfel as Don Giovanni.

Thomas Hampson as Don Giovanni.

Hei-Kyung Hong as Zerlina,   Cheryl Studer as Donna Anna.
Bryn Terfel as Don Giovanni.

Solveig Kringelborn as Donna Elvira, Bryn Terfel as Don Giovanni.

Die Zauberflöte

Act 1, scene 1.

Mary Dunleavy as the
Queen of the Night.

The final scene of *Die Zauberflöte*.

and a more human dramatic pace, he sped up opera seria to give it a dramatic shot in the arm that it would otherwise have lacked. Combine this notion with the addition of the choruses, the consistent use of instrumental color in the service of emotional expression, the sure musical trajectory leading into the two quasi finales, and the musical characterizations that I will examine more fully below, and the result truly is a new and improved brand of opera seria, Mozart style.

Until recently, this fact actually proved the greatest stumbling block to a modern appreciation of *Tito*. Mozart is one of those composers whose reputation for greatness rests to a large degree on his enlargement of existing forms, his ability to compose on the hugest scale, and his well-known desire always to write as lavishly as possible in every genre and circumstance. Here is the exception that proves the rule, for in creating a modern breed of opera seria, what Mozart needed to do was not expand the medium still further but rather pack the opera as compactly as possible so that the obligatory great moments, those big, long character numbers for Vitellia, Sextus, and Titus, stand out in high relief without stopping the opera's ongoing momentum dead in its tracks.

In *Tito*, Mozart achieves greatness not just by doing what he had done before, but rather by sensitively selecting only those elements of his personal style that he could most readily adapt to meet the needs of this particular subject and genre while preserving its fundamental dignity, austerity and simplicity. Despite his much-lauded ability to synthesize elements from many different schools and styles, Mozart never in his life created musical hybrids consisting of a random hodgepodge of incompatible elements, and he certainly wasn't about to start now.

Music and Characters

Overture

Aside from the fact that the end of the entire opera resembles that of the overture, there are no significant anticipations of things to come in this opening, very grand orchestral prelude. In fact, it has hardly any major themes at all. In the first book of this two-volume series, covering Mozart's instrumental music, I pointed out that one of the fundamental ways that music can sound big and formal is by building itself up from small harmonic and rhythmic formulas, and avoiding long-limbed, lyrical tunes that inevitably suggest the scale of the human voice. The overture to *Tito* does just that, resembling in this respect the first movement of the "Jupiter" Symphony and several movements in the "Haffner" and "Posthorn" serenades.

After some initial trumpet-and-drum march music, the essence of the piece consists of five staccato notes alternating with loud outbursts, followed by a big pileup of scales in the strings. Mozart takes these ideas (and a few others for contrast) through a number of harmonic turns, including some anguished outbursts in minor keys. There's none of the madcap lunacy of the comic operas, and the stately pace accurately anticipates that of the opera itself. Throughout, the orchestration remains unusually full, with the various orchestral sections pitted against each other in contrasting tonal blocks. Although the overture comes to a full stop, and the actual opera begins with simple recitative rather than an action number, you will notice that the dialogue picks up the conversation in the middle no less effectively than in the previous three operas.

Titus

One of the problems some people have with this opera concerns the personality of the title character: he hasn't much of one. Actually, that's not entirely true. It's just that most of his harsh or negative feelings fly by in secco recitative, while Mozart musically illustrates only his kinder, gentler side, which in any case dominates him to an extent that crowds out much room for contrast. Even so, his three arias aren't the same, and we have already noted how Mozart takes care to give musical voice to his loving and benevolent relationship with the people of Rome, to place Titus the public figure in the proper context.

One quality that distinguishes opera seria from comic opera, in Mozart at least, is the fact that arias tend to fall into fairly clear-cut types, each expressive of a particular mood or situation, and these archetypes tend to remain constant from character to character. For example, in his first solo, "Del più sublime soglio" (No. 6), Titus describes how his greatest pleasure lies in doing good works. The orchestration is identical, and the tone quite similar, to Vitellia's first aria, "Deh se piacer" (No. 2), in which she tells Sextus that if he wishes to please her, he must obey her command to kill Titus without question. Now obviously these two people are, to put it mildly, operating from opposite sides of the moral compass, but what matters is that both arias express the idea "This is what pleases me most." The sentiments are identical, even if the objects of pleasure differ radically.

The same procedure is followed in Titus's second aria, "Ah, se fosse intorno" (No. 8). There he expresses his appreciation for those who speak to him with honesty (Servilia, whom he wants to marry, has just confessed that she loves Annius). So later on, when Annius (in "Tu fosti tradito") asks Titus for mercy on behalf of Servilia's brother Sextus, the sincerity of his plea elicits a correspondingly similar instrumental setting, despite Titus's initial and quite reasonable anger. Annius, by way of clarification, is a soprano but not a castrato (the role was taken by a female singer then, as now). If you concluded from his first two arias that Titus has no independent existence of his own, you would be largely correct, because he sees himself exclusively as a public figure. He represents the best qualities of the Roman people that he rules, and has completely subordinated his personal feelings to his sense of duty.

Mozart does, however, offer two further glimpses of Titus the person rather than the icon. First, immediately following Annius's aria, Titus has a long accompanied recitative (strings only, and not numbered in the score) in which he reacts with horror at the suggestion that he consider mercy and only gradually gains control of himself. As he does so, the accompaniment thins out, becoming at last dry recitative. So he is human after all, Mozart seems to say, his bland exterior the result of tight self-discipline. Then, after his encounter with Sextus and ultimate decision to forgive him, Titus cuts loose with "Se all'impero" (No. 20), an extremely impressive aria in which he expresses his philosophy of life: if severity is what the job requires, he'd rather relinquish it than be obeyed out of fear instead of love.

For this bravura aria, Mozart adopts the baroque *da capo* (repeat) form, which simply means a big A section, a contrasting B section (here much slower), and a reprise of A, intensified by the singer's improvised ornamentation of the vocal line. In this case, Mozart writes out the repeat and provides his own embellishments. The tone of the outer sections is extremely heroic. All the goodness in Titus's character shines forth in this comparatively lengthy (five minute) piece, composed in a style whose old-fashioned solidity seems to echo the similarly timeless moral code being expressed. Because he is as much a symbol as a person, the character of Titus never arouses the interest of, say, Don Giovanni, but there's more to him than many commentators seem willing to grant. All that's necessary is attentive listening, a close reading of the text, and a little leeway in giving Mozart credit for knowing what he is doing.

Sextus

Despite being the title character, Titus is not the opera's male lead. Sextus, the castrato role, is. In classic opera-seria fashion, he begins the opera tormented by the conflict between love and duty, and that is how he remains until the very end, when Titus pardons him for his treason. This musically happy state of affairs (for the audience, if not for Sextus) earns him two of the opera's most important arias. The first is the absolutely thrilling "Parto, parto" (No. 9), which employs another tried–and-true baroque device: that of having a concertante instrumental solo mirroring and embroidering the vocal line. Mozart was fortunate to have Anton Stadler, his Viennese friend and the greatest clarinetist of the day, with him in Prague for the premiere performances, and so he featured the wind virtuoso both here and in Vitellia's great aria, "Non più di fiori."

If you have been listening to these works in sequence, you may recall a famous early example of this type of writing: Konstanze's "Marten aller Arten" from *The Abduction from the Seragio.* Even longer in length than this piece, and with four solo instruments instead of one, the language of opera seria sat somewhat uneasily in that aria next to the simpler, comic elements of singspiel. If you compare that setting to this one, you will hear immediately how much more naturally "Parto, parto" fits into the larger scheme of the opera as a whole. In it, Sextus agrees to kill Titus even though he risks his life, honor, and happiness, all for the love of Vitellia.

The solo clarinet sings poignantly of Sextus's longing for her, but more importantly, this aria represents the first real explosion of violent emotion encountered thus far. As Sextus's agitation increases, so does the tempo of the music and the elaborate vocal coloratura evocative of his passion—all the more effective for having been so long delayed.

In act 2, Sextus has the even more moving rondo "Deh, per questo istante solo" (No. 19). Here he touchingly asks Titus, to whom he has confessed his guilt without betraying Vitellia, for a last kind glance before sending him off to meet his death. The scoring, by the way, is the same as in his opening duet with Vitellia, "Come ti piace" (No. 1), where he also asks for a "sweet glance" as a reward for his devotion to her. I wouldn't go so far as to even suggest that Mozart is writing "glance" music. The point is that in both situations, Sextus is suffering under great emotional strain (as is Vitellia in No. 1), torn as he is between love and duty, and so this logically calls forth an identically textured musical setting. Mozart is always attentive to this sort of detail, even when one cannot say, as with his use of clarinets, that the scoring has a consistent meaning beyond this particular work.

Vitellia

Certainly one of the most thoroughly repulsive characters (morally speaking) in all of opera, Vitellia loves Titus and wants him dead because he won't marry her. Of course, as soon as she sends Sextus off to do the dastardly deed, Titus decides to ask for her hand after all, but it's too late to stop the long-planned rebellion and assassination plot. In act 1, then, Vitellia lusts for revenge even as Sextus lusts for her. In act 2, she's guilt-stricken over the fact that Sextus, who has failed to kill Titus, is ready to die for her, and she ultimately confesses her guilt in what everyone agrees is one of Mozart's most moving arias: "Non più di fiori,"

No. 23. Prior to this, and aside from her participation in a few of the ensembles—especially the impressive act 1 trio "Vengo! Aspettate!"—she sings the relatively placid "Deh se piacer" (No. 2), telling Sextus that if he loves and wants to please her, then he must do her bidding with out question. Like so many arias in *Tito,* this first one (although not called a rondo), employs two tempos, first slow, then fast. This format allows Mozart to create a rush of energy within all of the longer numbers, and it represents a sort of opera seria analogue to the action music so frequently encountered in the comedies.

The entire opera, however, truly culminates in Vitellia's final rondo, even though a bit more music necessarily follows to provide the formal resolution. It's the longest aria in the whole work (about eight minutes) and certainly the most expressive. The essence of the text is a sad farewell to Vitellia's dreams of empire and marriage. The music shares the idea of parting with Sextus's "Parto, parto," and accordingly, its clarinet solo (here a basset horn, which has a lower range and a darker sound better suited to the music's frequent excursions to despairing, minor-key tonalities). You may also hear in Vitellia's vocal line the same wide-ranging leaps that Mozart gave to Fiordiligi, the most opera seria–like character in *Così fan tutte.* But there is nothing comic about Vitellia, no exaggeration of the type that makes Fiordiligi's "Come scoglio" such a wonderful example of musical parody. Indeed, it's entirely typical of Mozart that he gives the opera's most horrible character the most moving and sympathetic music to sing.

The remaining three roles have only four relatively brief arias among them, all in the second act, and they don't require discussion in detail. Compared to the comedies, *La Clemenza di Tito* is an uncomplicated piece, but I think you can see that Mozart composed it with the same inner logic and attention to detail as he did those larger, more complex works (and despite the fact that he apparently had help writing the simple recitatives so as to be ready for the premiere).

It's absurd to think that Mozart, who was seriously looking for work and always in financial trouble, would treat with disdain a commission to write an opera for a royal coronation. In fact, just about the only comment we have from Mozart about the piece is "I did my best." Leaving aside for the moment the inherent wisdom of taking him at his word, it's foolish to judge *Tito* by standards that it never adopts in the first place. If it does not achieve the popularity of the great comedies, it won't be because the music isn't worthy but because operas about subjects like mercy will never attract as large an audience as operas about sex and human frailty. This is perfectly natural, as long as one understands that good music about mercy can be every bit as entertaining and rewarding in its own way.

Die Zauberflöte (The Magic Flute) *1791*

Introduction

The Magic Flute was conceived as genuine, popular entertainment for the masses, and in this respect it has certainly dated. Perhaps no other opera libretto in the repertoire is at once so silly and so sublime, and only the strength of Mozart's music, which is wholly sublime, has kept it alive. Indeed, it has done more than that: it has exercised a fascination on writers, composers, and painters as diverse as Goethe (who wrote a sequel), Marion Zimmer Bradley (who wrote a science fiction novel explaining the background), Wagner (in *Parsifal*), Richard Strauss (in *Die Frau ohne Schatten*), Michael Tippett (in *The Midsummer Marriage*), and Marc Chagall (who designed the sets for a production at the Metropolitan Opera). Far and away the richest singspiel ever written, musically speaking, as well as the most lavish orchestral composition that Mozart ever set down on paper, it was first performed on September 30, 1791. Only a few weeks later, Mozart was dead.

To find similar examples of this strangely compelling mixture of high and low art, of the popular and the erudite, one would have to turn to the works of Shakespeare, whose play *The Tempest* quite possibly served as a model for Mozart's librettist, the impresario Emanuel Schikaneder (who also sang the role of Papageno at the premiere). Schikaneder was a noted Shakespearean actor and knew the Bard well (as most likely did Mozart). Both *The Tempest* and *The Magic Flute* feature a benevolent magician (Prospero and Sarastro respectively) arranging events so as to consecrate the union of a young couple thrown together in supernatural circumstances. Both include important parts for an evil slave nominally working on the magician's behalf (Caliban/Monostatos), and in both cases the magician subjects the young couple to a series of tests, "lest too light winning make the prize light," as Prospero puts it in the play.

This, then, is essentially the plot of *The Magic Flute,* although Schikaneder and Mozart toss in all kinds of asides, diversions, and subplots (as does Shakespeare, albeit differently) along the way. Two points about the opera need to be dealt with up front: its racism (Monostatos is the nasty black guy who wants the nice white girl) and its misogyny (Sorastro and crew spout all kinds of nonsense about the weakness and evil of women). Certainly one can't accuse Mozart of cultivating this last sentiment: almost all of his greatest and most sympathetic operatic characters (including those in this very work) are women, some of them—Konstanze in *The Abduction from the Seraglio,* for example—incomparably more heroic and noble than the men. And like the similarly stereotyped character of Shylock in Shakespeare's *The Merchant of Venice,* the offensive racial element in *The Magic Flute* attests to the common Viennese prejudices of a bygone (or so one hopes) age.

Indeed, the character of Shylock looms large here as well, because Monostatos sings an aria in act 2 (No. 13) that almost quotes the Shakespearean character's famous "Hath not a Jew" speech. "Everyone feels love's joy," Monostatos says, "but because I am black and therefore a horrid sight, I must separate myself from love. Was I not given a heart? Am I not made of flesh and blood?" Of course he remains, like Shylock, one of the bad guys, but as in Shakespeare, Mozart and his colleague at least

#	Title	Flutes	Oboes	Clarinets	Bassoons	Horns	Trumpets	Timpani	Trombones
	Die Zauberflöte: Quick Reference								
				Orchestration (in Addition to Strings)					
	Act 1								
1	Introduction: Zu Hilfe!	2	2	2	2	2	2	yes	
2	Aria: Der Vogelfänger bin ich ja		2		2	2			
3	Aria: Dies Bildniss ist bezaubernd schön			2	2	2			
4	Aria: O zitt're nicht, mein lieber Sohn		2		2	2			
5	Quintet: Hm hm hm		2	2	2	2			
6	Trio: Du feines Täubchen, nur herein	1	2		2	2			
7	Duet: Bei Männern, welche Liebe fühlen			2	2	2			
8	Finale: Zum Ziele führt dich diese Bahn	2	2	2	2	2	2	yes + glock.	3
	Act 2								
9	March of the Priests	1		2	2	2			3
9a	The thrice repeated chord	2	2	basset horns	2	2	2		3
10	Aria w/Chorus: O Isis und Osiris				2				3
11	Duet: Bewahret euch vor Weiberstücken	2	2	2	2	2	2	yes	3
12	Quintet: Wie? Ihr an diesem Schreckensort	2	2		2	2	2	yes	3
13	Aria: Alles fühlt der Liebe Freuden	1 + piccolo		2	2				
14	Aria: Der Hölle Rache kocht in meinem Herzen	2	2		2	2	2	yes	
15	Aria: In diesen heil'gen Hallen	2			2	2			
16	Trio: Seid uns zum zweiten Mal willkommen	2			2				
17	Aria: Ah, ich fühl's, es ist verschwunden	1	1		1				
18	Chorus: O Isis und Osiris	2	2		2	2	2		3
19	Trio: Soll ich dich, Theurer, nicht mehr sehn		2		2				
20	Aria: Ein Mädchen oder Weibchen	1	2		2	2		glocken-spiel	
21	Finale: Bald prangt, den Morgen zu verkünden	2	2	2	2	2	2	yes + glock.	3

Table of Individual Numbers and Orchestration

give Monostatos a sympathetic glance before falling back on social convention. Indeed the depth of characterization of the human/nonmagical roles in *The Magic Flute,* Pamina in particular, achieves the same level of emotional realism as in the great Italian comedies, while the grandeur of the ceremonial scenes equals the depth and outdoes the solemnity of anything in *Idomeneo* or *La clemenza di Tito.*

Another potential stumbling block to a modern appreciation of the opera stems from its endlessly discussed links to the movement known as Freemasonry. You don't have to know anything about this to enjoy the music, but commentators on the opera often delight in pointing out obscure symbolic correspondences between its dramaturgy and Masonic ritual (both Mozart and Schikaneder were Freemasons), and this sometimes creates the impression among listeners that the opera must mean more to people who possess this arcane knowledge than it does to those who do not. Frankly, I can't imagine anything more untrue, uninteresting, and musically irrelevant. Essentially the Men's Club of the Enlightenment, all you need to know about the Freemasons is that they were big on the number three (hence the opera's three ladies, three boys, thrice-repeated chords, and so forth), and that some of the ritual gobbledygook of Sarastro's quasi-religious society purportedly derives from Masonic mythology. Next subject, please.

Practically speaking, the real difficulty for non–German speakers lies in the reams of dialogue, often thankfully cut in actual performance, between the various numbers. After all, the plot makes little sense irrespective of the language employed, so one would think that translations would at least try to be straightforwardly comprehensible rather than poetic and obscure, but many of them fall into the latter trap. This fact, the Masonic business, and the perversity of opera producers the world over often conspire to drown the clarity and expressive directness of Mozart's contribution in linguistic, pseudo-philosophical, and theatrical clutter. Considering that the finales of both acts contain the longest, most varied, and most exciting stretches of continuous music that Mozart ever wrote in an opera, totaling some fifty minutes (twenty minutes for act 1 and thirty minutes for act 2, on average), this is more than unfortunate. Of course, that's what makes recordings so useful.

If you take a moment to look at the table of individual numbers and orchestration, you will see both familiar instrumental combinations and new discoveries. In an opera with a strong love interest, one naturally finds Mozart's characteristic sounds of sweet melancholy and yearning—namely, pairs of clarinets, bassoons, and horns (with optional flutes)—right from Tamino's first aria, "Dies Bildness" (No. 3). This special tone color also dominates the entire opening scene of the act 2 finale, in which the three boys console Pamina, who is distraught at the thought that Tamino might have abandoned her. Mozart makes great use of the solemn sounds of trombones in the temple scenes involving Sarastro, and they serve the same purpose as in *Idomeneo* and, especially, *Don Giovanni,* where their imposing tone adds weight to the supernatural happenings in that opera's finale.

Basset horns, those lovely, low-pitched members of the clarinet family, also figure prominently at these moments. You met them previously in *The Abduction from the Seraglio* and *La clemenza di Tito.* The Moor Monostatos, a latter-day Osmin (the Pasha's servant in *The Abduction*), gets the sole aria that includes a piccolo, an exotic instrument in those days associated with Turkish or Oriental music. Mozart's glockenspiel (a keyboard instrument closer to the modern celesta than to the more familiar mallet model) provides the voice of Papageno's magic bells. As for the flute named in the title, it appears in the finales of both acts with important solos, especially in Tamino's scene in act 1, "Wie stark ist nicht dein Zauberton." The orchestration under the solo flute in its act 2 march (played during the Trial by Fire) is particularly wonderful: Mozart accompanies the melody with soft horns, trumpets, trombones, and timpani.

Indeed, the instrumentation in *The Magic Flute* offers so clear a synthesis of all that Mozart has learned in his previous operas (even the muted trumpets and timpani from the march music in *Idomeneo* make a brief appearance) that one could be forgiven for mistaking it as the work of a much older composer, a serene reflection on a lifetime of musical experience. There's an autumnal wisdom to much of the music, a purity of utterance that has nothing to do with our *ex post facto* knowledge of Mozart's death shortly after the premiere (or any foolishness about his "premonitions" in this regard). The honest truth is that the entire work is, effectively, one giant ending—the conclusion of a process that began long before the actions that take place on stage.

In a sense this observation is true of all of the operas considered thus far. The great Italian comedies, for example, take place in a single day and represent a resolution of longstanding conflicts and relationship problems. The difference, though, is that in those operas, the audience is always told all that it needs to know about how the characters came to be involved in the situations in which they are found. In *Don Giovanni,* for example, Donna Elvira has been jilted by Giovanni previously, but the audience knows what her relationship to him was, and aside from her, all of the other goings-on in the opera are fresh encounters between the characters, requiring no background knowledge. *Così fan tutte* lives entirely in the present: Mozart frames the whole substance of the drama in the opening few minutes. Even *The Marriage of Figaro,* the story of which is technically a sequel to *The Barber of Seville,* requires no familiarity with prior events to make perfect sense when taken on its own. *The Magic Flute* is different.

Before the curtain goes up, Pamina has already been kidnapped by Sarastro (although her mother, the Queen of the Night, seems to have no trouble reaching her when she needs to). Her father is long gone, and once possessed a magical talisman called a "sun circle" (whatever that is), which Sarastro took from him. Tamino is a prince from someplace or other, far from home, being chased by a giant serpent when the opera opens, we know not why. Papageno is a . . . well . . . we're not quite sure exactly what he is. Marion Zimmer Bradley, in her sci-fi/fantasy novel *Night's Daughter*, suggests experiments in human-animal cross-breading and genetic manipulation—surely as sensible a description of Papageno as any. He's a good guy but a servant of the Queen, who is evil, while Monostatos is a bad guy and a servant of Sarastro, who is good. How Sarastro and the Queen came to be neighbors in the first place is anyone's guess. We do at least know why they are enemies: Sarastro has Mr. Night's sun circle.

What attracted Mozart to this seemingly incoherent story that only picks up the tale at the end, and that keeps its audience mystified throughout? The question provides its own answer. It falls to the music to make clear what the words do not; to give these characters a repertoire, and thus a history, of emotions and feelings; to reveal what the characters are thinking and to interpret their actions; and most importantly, to give to this crazy story a satisfying finale. What great composer could resist taking upon himself the challenge that Mozart rises to here: the freedom to define the terms of the drama almost exclusively through the music and, moreover, to do it in a setting that offers the broadest exposure to a wide audience of all ages and classes of society? More than any other of his stage works, *The Magic Flute* gave Mozart his biggest and best chance to be true to himself, at the same time offering the infinitely sweeter opportunity to prove that his greatest music could also be his most popular and successful.

And so with his usual intelligence, aided perhaps by that unconscious instinct that only accompanies true genius, Mozart composed a score that is as much a musical summing up and synthesis of prior experience as is the actual story. But because Mozart enjoys the luxury of being ruthlessly logical in his own domain, especially when the plot is whizzing nonsensically about all over the map, he once again achieves that necessary suspension of disbelief that draws us into the world of his characters and makes us feel what they feel. You have already heard him give psychological depth and realism to the stock personalities that inhabit comic opera, and breathe life into the statuesque icons of opera seria. Now he reveals, through his own inimitable combination of warmth, seriousness, and humor, that even the most irrational and outrageous of fairy tales has at its core a very human heart.

Music and Characters *

Overture

The overture tells the audience exactly what to expect for the next couple of hours, although it only quotes at its very center one significant motive from the opera: the thrice-repeated chord (No. 9a). This, together with the gorgeously solemn opening, featuring the trombones from the very first gesture, represents Sarastro's realm. The balance of the movement is a series of fugatos for strings and winds alternating with vigorous rhythmic outbursts from the full orchestra. (A *fugato* is simply a single tune

---

* Unlike the other commentaries on the operas, which simply take note of each important character in turn, this one on The Magic Flute demands a slightly different approach. There are in fact three different character types, each distinguished by a specific musical style, and so the following discussion considers each in turn.

played in sequence by any number of instrumental voices, with staggered entrances occurring every few bars so that the tune piles up on itself. If an entire piece is written in strict fugato style, it may well be called a *fugue*.)

This kind of contrapuntal writing has a reputation for being very learned, as indeed it is, since the ear automatically recognizes and appreciates the complexity inherent in several independent voices presented in linear fashion, cooperating to create a harmonious whole while retaining their individual rhythmic and thematic identities. But this is only half the story, because the theme (or *subject*) of this contrapuntal display is as primitive-sounding a folklike tune as "Twinkle, Twinkle, Little Star" (which Mozart turned into one of his best known set of piano variations). In other words, the overture's quick allegro sections offer a simultaneous mix of the simple and sophisticated, the funny and the serious, the anxious and the joyous.

The overture's fugato sections, combined with the slow music at the beginning and the thrice-repeated chord in the middle, more completely describe Mozart's musical procedure in this opera than words ever can, and he serves up this conceptual preview in less than six minutes. It provides yet another example of Mozart's ability to convey a great deal of information in a very short span of time. More importantly, it is a reminder that a musical idea need not necessarily be just the first tune that is heard on the musical surface, but rather the way that the composer presents and develops his thematic material. Over the next two acts, you will encounter more than one instance of simple or familiar ideas treated in surprising and subtle ways, and the process begins right here.

Supernatural/Magical Characters: Sarastro and the Queen of the Night

Although these two characters fall into the same general category, their musical portraits are as different as—well—night and day. Sarastro belongs to a long line of operatic magicians, priests, holy hermits, wise men, and oracles. From a purely dramaturgical point of view, he has basically the same function as Pasha Selim in *The Abduction from the Seraglio,* being more an element of the plot than a fully developed character in his own right. Unlike the Pasha, however, he actually gets to sing, and this presents Mozart with a real problem. In music, as with so many arts, "good" is often synonymous with "boring." How can Mozart convey the character's transcendental saintliness without putting his audience to sleep? The answer has two principal components.

First, aside from brief contributions to the two finales, Mozart bunches most of Sarastro's music into the first three (yes, three) numbers of act 2. This gets him out of the way as quickly as possible, while the audience is still fresh (let us not be naïve and underestimate the importance of factors like this in performance, or Mozart's shrewdness in this regard). All three pieces (Nos. 9, 9a, and 10) are slow and grand, sharing the same basic orchestral coloration (basset horns and trombones), and each conveys a sense of timeless majesty, although in an individual way. They must have particularly pleased the Masonic contingent in the audience. Of the two orchestral numbers, "The March of the Priests" (No. 9) opens the act (and sounds suspiciously like the Canadian national anthem "O Canada.") It is a solemn processional. Next follows the thrice-repeated chord (No. 9a), a ritual summons to action. Sarastro then speaks at some length, and finally sings No. 10, the hymn-with-chorus "O Isis und Osiris" (scored for an atmospheric accompaniment of basset horns, bassoons, trombones, violas, and cellos).

Mozart was a master at suggesting largeness of scale in a very short span of time. All of these numbers are brief, but note how much more impressive it is to have three smaller but cleanly differentiated items in a row instead of a single long but perhaps ultimately boring one. Sarastro dominates the proceedings as the only soloist, but in reality the part is very tiny and successfully presents the character not so much as an individual but rather as the voice of a philosophical ideal. Indeed, this sort of musical portrayal of an entire community of belief hasn't been seen since the great choral scenes in *Idomeneo*, only here Mozart has found a way to integrate this monumental and very abstract collective character into the overall dramatic flow.

Among the gems of wisdom concerning women that come from Sarastro, the icon of enlightenment and goodness, is this one, offered to Pamina at the end of act 1:

> A man must direct your hearts,
> Because without him, every woman
> Steps beyond her accustomed place.

The particular woman in question is the Queen of the Night, Pamina's mother, and Mozart makes no bones about the fact that evil is much, much more fun in a musical setting than good. Indeed, one of strangest and most seemingly contradictory facts about this deliberately confusing story is that Sarastro, who manages the realm of the sun and of light, is a bass whose orchestration is invariably dark and heavy, while the Queen of the Night, ruler of darkness, is a high soprano whose orchestration is bright and brilliant. Naturally there's a profound, deeply meaningful and symbolic reason why this is so. I just have no idea what it is.

Anyway, this portrait makes a huge impression out of all proportion to its actual size: the Queen sings only two arias and a few lines in the finale of act 2, actually less than ten minutes of music in all. But what arias they are! For many listeners, this role provides the main reason for listening to the whole opera. Entire careers can be built on a singer's ability to hit those nearly impossible high Fs with consistency and precision. Clearly this is a larger-than-life character, and the vocal pyrotechnics that so dazzle the audience belong to the world of opera seria, where virtuosity of this sort serves as an extension of the emotional intensity of expression. As befits a character whose only thought is vengeance, Mozart denies the Queen the soft tones of clarinets in both of these big solos. With her heroic first aria, "O zitt're nicht" (No. 4), she fires Tamino with the necessary resolve to go off and rescue Pamina from Sarastro.

In her terrifyingly vicious second aria, "Der Hölle Rache" (No. 14), Mozart adds trumpets and timpani, and the fireworks really begin. The Queen has just appeared before Pamina and given her a dagger, ordering her to murder Sarastro and return the stolen sun circle—or else. You can hear this, arguably the most famous aria ever written for high coloratura soprano, on track 15 of the included CD. Here are the words:

Der Hölle Rache kocht in meinem Herzen,	Hellish fury brews in my heart,
Tod und Verzweiflung flammet um mich her!	Flaming death and woe surround me!
Fühlt nicht durch dich Sarastro Todesschmerzen,	If you do not make Sarastro feel the Agony of death,
So bist du meine Tochter nimmermehr.	Then you will never more be my daughter.
Verstoßen sei auf ewig,	You will be cut off forever,
Verlassen sei auf ewig,	You will be forsaken forever,

Zertrümmert sei'n auf ewig	You will be severed forever
Alle Bande der Natur	From all natural bonds,
Wenn nicht durch dich	If Sarastro is not vanquished
Sarastro wird erblassen!	By your hand!
Hört, Rachegötter,	Hear, Gods of Vengeance,
Hört der Mutter Schwur!	Hear a mother's oath!

The handling of the orchestra in this aria really is marvelous, being a classic case of music that impresses as loud but in fact spends most of its time at quieter dynamic levels so as not to cover the voice. Mozart achieves this effect through careful use of accent and by placing violent explosions for the full orchestra between the singer's phrases. Pay special attention to the use of flutes when the voice soars up into the stratosphere: they merge with the vocal timbre to create a sound that is positively unearthly, setting the seal on the audience's impression of the Queen as a being of supernatural power.

The very next number in the opera is Sarastro's only true solo aria, "In diesen heil'gen Hallen" (No. 15), a beautiful largo that constitutes the exact opposite of what was just heard, even as it similarly avoids the use of clarinets (its subject is not love, but the virtue of mercy and forgiveness). Pamina has confessed what her mother has ordered her to do, and Sarastro assures her that he is not intimidated or angry, because in his temple vengeance is unknown. It almost makes you wish that he might consider permitting a tiny bit of vengeance now and then just to perk things up, but we get the point, which is to offer a marked contrast between the two characters. Indeed, this aria and the music of the first three numbers in act 2 constitute perhaps the finest "religious" music that Mozart ever wrote: it has depth, sincerity, and a timeless quality that recalls the early Mass settings of composers such as Palestrina and Victoria, even though the style is very different.

The violent contrast between Sarastro and the Queen of the Night further emphasizes an important fact about her: she is completely alone, even isolated, her power dwindling, and so her two appearances represent a desperate last stand. Mozart enlarges upon this idea in the further contrast between the music of the Three Ladies, who work for the Queen, and the Three Boys, who assist Sarastro. The Ladies bicker among themselves, after their rescue of Tamino in the opera's first scene, while the boys act as if always of one mind, highlighting the opposition of self-interest on the one hand and the communal values of harmony and cooperation on the other.

The two trios, of Ladies and Boys, exist solely as personifications of the wills of their respective masters. All of the other characters with the exception of Monostatos, who switches sides late in the opera, are on Sarastro's side. I strongly suspect that the idea of creating an orchestral identity for the Queen's realm would have appealed to Mozart, for reasons of both symmetry and contrast. However, perhaps out of considerations of economy and time, the audience does not see corresponding scenes taking place in her court. So Mozart makes her music as strong and vivid as possible, packing as much punch as he can into her brief appearances. The result: her passion temporarily wins the musical battles, but Sarastro's calm deliberation ultimately wins the war.

Human/Animal Creatures: Papageno and Papagena

Papagena doesn't show up until the end of act 2 (before that she is a mysterious old woman), so most of these remarks concern the half-man, half-bird Papageno. His music bears a loose resemblance to all of Mozart's tonal portraits of the lower classes. It is rustic and folksy, scored for the traditional pastoral combination of flutes and oboes, and although Papageno's numbers, "Der Vogelfänger" and "Ein Mädchen oder Weibchen" (Nos. 2 and 20), are called arias, they take the form of simple strophic songs. Most discussions of the opera present Papageno's music as a direct appeal to the masses on the part of Mozart and Schikaneder. Certainly these "pop songs" set your toes tapping, but the notion that they represent a deliberate attempt to pander to the taste of a certain class of listener has always struck me as a touch condescending, not to mention naïve. After all, what are those supposedly low-class folks to make of the remaining two and a half hours of music?

In fact, my own experience with the opera, having seen it with many people who have little or no familiarity with the genre, is that their impression is the same as everyone else's. Papageno's music is cute, but it's the Queen of the Night who really blows them away. The "class differentiation" theory of any art, but especially music, usually has very little to do with the art itself and everything to do with commentators looking for neat categories that conform to prior assumptions. Were the lower classes in Shakespeare's day only able to enjoy the opening comic scene of *Julius Caesar* (and were the wealthy and educated bored by it), or did everyone simply enjoy the full range of the drama—the comedy and the tragedy, the poetry and the prose—equally? The answer, which I hope is obvious, suggests that the best way to understand what Mozart is doing with Papageno and Papagena is not to treat them as a foreign element intruding on the world of genuine opera but rather to look at their music in context. If you do this, you can make some very telling observations.

Papageno's first aria is one of those "This is who I am" numbers that listeners familiar with, say, Gilbert and Sullivan's operettas will recognize immediately: "I am the Captain of the Pinafore," "I'm Called Little Buttercup," "A Wandering Minstrel I," and so forth. Both this song and his famous duet with Papagena in the finale of act 2 make great play with nonsense syllables (*Heissa hopsassa* and *pa pa pa* respectively). Papageno's second aria tinkles delightfully to the accompaniment of the glockenspiel, just like a music box. What Mozart has written, in fact, isn't mere "peasant" music. These are nursery tunes. Papageno is, musically speaking, a child. His insistence that he is as human as Tamino comes across with exactly the same bravado as when a child insists, "I *am* grown up!" so as to receive the same privileges and respect as the real adults.

Now take this idea one step further. The character is half man, half bird—in reality nothing more than a giant, cuddly pet personified as a big child. Indeed, seen from this viewpoint he is probably the most logical character in the entire opera. He trusts unquestioningly, constantly seeks approval and affection, instinctively yearns for the company of his own kind, and can't keep still or quiet for two seconds at a time, just like a little boy. And the other characters react to him exactly as one does to a rambunctious child: with a smile of indulgence, an occasional touch of corrective discipline, and a reward when he obeys, even if his behavior hasn't been absolutely perfect.

So yes, Papageno's music *might* have appealed most strongly to one segment of the audience more than other bits of the opera, but the important point is that it perfectly describes the character that the *entire* audience sees on stage. I think it far more likely that Mozart and Schikaneder intended Papageno, along with the opera as a whole, to speak directly to "children of all ages" as a single, unified work, just as adults tend to enjoy Prokofiev's *Peter and the Wolf* as much as their kids do. Good, clean fun and catchy tunes will always have universal appeal, and reminders of the simple joys of childhood need not be directed at one social class in preference to another.

Human Beings: Tamino and Pamina (and One Surprise)

With Tamino and Pamina, audiences are on familiar Mozartean ground. As the only two normal human characters, as well as boyfriend and girlfriend, they get the full musical "love" treatment, and this means above all scoring that includes clarinets. Tamino's first aria, "Dies Bildniss" (No. 3), drives the point home immediately. He takes one look at Pamina's portrait, exclaims, "This picture is enchantingly beautiful," and falls in love. Another logically absurd moment in an opera full of them, we never question Tamino's commitment or sincerity. Mozart's music says that he's in love, and that's that. This is just one of those things that opera can do so well, as compared to just about any other form of theater. Mozart's setting strikingly recalls the mood of Ferrando's "Un'aura amorosa" from *Così fan tutte.*

Pamina's first number is a duet with Papageno, "Bei Männern" (No. 7), with scoring exactly the same as in Tamino's first aria, as is the intent of the text: "We want to enjoy love, and we live through love alone." However Pamina's big solo, "Ach, ich fühl's" (No. 17), expresses not yearning for love but rather despair: it is one of the great moments of deep pathos in vocal music, requiring the smoothest legato and precise breath control from the singer. Here, the plaintive tone of the solo oboe best suits the setting. Contrast this aria with the emotionally comparable "Dove sono," sung by the Countess at a similar point in *The Marriage of Figaro* when she believes she has lost the love of her husband. Driven almost to madness and suicide by her grief, Pamina regains her reason, her hope, and her clarinets at the opening of the act 2 finale, when the Three Boys convince her that Tamino loves her still. And isn't it an especially delightful paradox that, despite Sarastro's best advice, the two most powerful and moving characters in the entire opera are both women?

The surprise in this portrait gallery is Monostatos, the evil Moor. He too is a person seeking love, and his short aria in act 2, "Alles fühlt der Liebe Freuden" (No. 13), in addition to the exotic piccolo already mentioned accordingly, also has clarinets. Mozart doesn't make a point of emphasizing them as he does in Tamino's or Pamina's music. As the tempo is swift, the dynamic level low, and the vocal line not at all lyrical, you may not notice them. But the sense of the text (although grotesquely stated) is essentially the same as the Pamina/Papageno duet (No. 7), even though the musical setting is a parody leaving no doubt as to the Moor's right to affect such feelings with respect to Pamina. Monostatos's voice part, a tenor like Tamino's, contributes further to this element of parody, but with all that (Mozart's music seems to say) *he is still a human being who needs love too,* however perverted. The logic and consistency of characterization here really is breathtaking.

I would like to conclude this discussion of *The Magic Flute* by returning for a moment to its Shakespearean range of reference and popular appeal. Here is an interesting musical fact: the entire opera contains only nine arias, two less than *La Clemenza di Tito,* for example, which is actually much shorter (taking into account the relative amount of dry recitative and dialogue in each work). In the three big Italian comedies, most of the principal characters can count on at least two arias each. Here the humans have only one apiece, while it is the Queen of the Night, Sarastro, and Papageno who each get two solo numbers. The remaining twelve pieces are either instrumental, choruses of some kind, or ensembles (and the two huge finales certainly belong in this latter category as well).

The conclusion is inescapable: *The Magic Flute* is not, first and foremost, a love story, any more than is *Idomeneo* or *La clemenza di Tito.* Like those works, it is an allegorical drama, probably the most easily digestible one ever written, but so different from the conventions of opera seria that it's difficult to believe that these three pieces, never mind the Italian comedies, are all the work of the same composer. However, just as the triviality of opera buffa challenged Mozart to make his characters come alive in a realistic way by introducing deeper emotional elements, so *The Magic Flute* can best be understood as a sort of "singspiel seria," in which the comic and the serious work hand in hand to deliver the opera's message with more color and variety than either could separately.

If you combine this fact with the clarity of Mozart's musical delineation of the three distinct character types outlined above, the result is a very unconventional work that some listeners find frustrating—not so much because the plot is silly, but because they tend to prefer one type of its music and have certain fixed expectations about what an opera should be about. In other words, the size and shape of the package can lead to false assumptions about the identity of the gift inside. Hard-core opera fanatics enjoy the Queen of the Night, Tamino, and Pamina. Papageno appeals to pet lovers, children, and fans of musical theater. Sarastro and his crew find favor with the choral-music and religious-oratorio crowd. In short, one's reaction to the piece is not so much a function (as some would have you believe) of cultural sophistication and social class, but simply of taste, personal preference, and as with *Tito,* a willingness to meet the work on its own terms.

So to claim that *The Magic Flute* is a musical grab bag would not only be wrong; it flies in the face of the very logic and consistency that define the opera's language in the first place. The best way to disprove this theory is to listen to the two finales, where Mozart proceeds to combine all of the various elements in a vast river of seamlessly flowing music in which nothing strikes the ear as incongruous. Any piece that covers as much ground as this one will prove disconcerting to those who prefer a more classically pure aesthetic (or one more closely wedded to accepted conventions). Certainly Mozart isn't alone among great opera composers in being able to satisfy both types of listener. In this respect he strongly resembles Verdi, whose work has room for the refinement and realism of *La traviata* at the same time as the sprawling imbroglio of coincidence and illogic that is *La forza del destino*.

There is nothing odd, then, when a composer creates an unusually wide range of characters within a plot structure operating on several different levels at once, for some listeners to enjoy certain aspects of the story and musical setting more than others. This is even truer when the most immediately sympathetic roles may not in fact be the most important ones in getting the work's primary message across. But just as few people today accuse Shakespeare of being a bad playwright because he allots such a big part in *Macbeth* to the *three* witches (was he also a Freemason?), so too it makes little sense to take Mozart to task in *The Magic Flute* for spending so much time on Papageno or Sarastro. In both cases, the real reason for any reservations stems not from the artists' inability to do their job properly, but rather from the reaction of individual spectators to the fact that they do it so well.

Part 2

Other Vocal Works

The Not-So-Great Operas

Apollo et Hyacinthus (1767)
Bastien und Bastienne (1768)
La finta semplice (1768)
Mitridate, re di Ponto (1770)
Ascanio in Alba (1771)
Lucio Silla (1772)
Il sogno de Scipione (1772)
La finta giardiniera (1775)
Il re pastore (1775)
Zaide (1779)
Der Schauspieldirektor (1786)

Mozart's mature operas are so well known and universally loved, and his reputation as a miraculous prodigy spewing out perfect masterpieces by the truckload so generally accepted, that it comes as something of a shock to realize that the majority of his operatic music is little known and almost totally ignored. This isn't because it's bad. It's just not great, comparatively speaking. Beyond that, from a practical perspective, opera is simply too complicated and expensive an enterprise to be able to afford big risks in reviving long neglected works, even by Mozart, unless motivated by real public demand or a reasonable certainty of artistic success.

Music is also unique among the arts in its reliance on the time factor. From the very beginning of his career, Mozart showed a real gift for vivid characterization in music, and if you take the time—lots of time—to get to know any of the above works as well as avid opera goers know the most famous ones, it will not be a difficult task to convince yourself that they are unjustly neglected. Some of them undoubtedly are. Virtually all of them contain flashes of greatness to come, have marvelous arias and ensembles, and offer plenty of opportunity for enjoyment, particularly on recordings, where you can determine the amount of time and attention to give them at your own convenience.

On the other hand, all of them are also deficient in qualities that are found in abundance in the operas from *Idomeneo* on, whether it's depth of characterization, control of dramatic momentum, treatment of the orchestra, length and variety of content, or just plain good storytelling. Composers in Mozart's day, writing operas on commission, were usually not given their choice of libretto. Most often, the story would be a familiar one that had been set many times previously, the ease of comparison to other settings being a prime means of determining the success of the new work and the composer's fitness for future assignments. Originality, as we now understand it, was not a desirable quality if this meant doing something different for its own sake.

The preeminence of singers in the musical hierarchy meant that each work had to be written (and rewritten) with their specific strengths and weaknesses in mind, and the same practical consideration held true with respect to the size and handling of the orchestra. It's no coincidence that Mozart's greatness as an opera composer dates from his period as a freelance composer, when he was able to judge the public taste himself and create works that he hoped would be both novel—true to his own vision of what opera should be—and also popular with his audiences. He was very good at achieving his first two aims, less good at the third, but obviously there's no need to worry about that now, and his career was by no means characterized by neglect at the highest and most prestigious levels of society. In fact, when Mozart died so prematurely, he was doing well critically and artistically, if not always financially.

In addition, for those who are interested and want to understand the "Mozart phenomenon" in greater depth, there's an undoubted fascination in spending some time with comparatively immature works, in order not just to understand better what makes the great ones so special but also to observe Mozart's artistic progress from one piece to the next. Listeners are fortunate that such works are available on recordings, for despite what many assume, not all artistic careers constitute a path of uninterrupted growth and development from beginning to end.

Mendelssohn, for example, a prodigy at least as gifted as Mozart, was artistically mature by his midteens and turned out works of widely varying quality for the remainder of his life. You will search in vain for the sort of continuous development and enlargement of vision that most take for granted in Mozart. Even more remarkable in an age of continuous self-borrowing (and wholesale thievery), there is not a single significant instance of Mozart's reusing material from an earlier opera in a later one, a fact that speaks volumes about his instinctive and very modern feeling for the integrity of his works as consistently conceived wholes.

I offer this brief survey of the lesser works to make it easier for you to determine your own most convenient point of entry. I also include the titles of an important aria or two that you may encounter from time to time in both live and recorded recitals. The vast majority of these are for the soprano/castrato lead roles. Unlike the discussions of the great operas, the focus here must necessarily involve a simple description of what these pieces are, rather than how they sound. On the other hand, if you like opera in the first place, know Mozart's best works, and have the time to sit down with the words and pay attention to the relationship between text and musical setting, then you already have all the tools that you need to get the most out of these early pieces.

Apollo et Hyacinthus

This "school drama" was the greatest hit of the 1767 academic season at Salzburg University. The story comes from Ovid, and the whole thing is in Latin—not that there's anything wrong with that. Virtually everyone who has heard it agrees that this roughly ninety-minute-long work is a remarkable achievement for an eleven-year-old—and that once is enough. It demonstrates that even at this age, Mozart had a good basic command of the musical language of his day. But then there are plenty of other Mozart works that reveal exactly the same thing and spend much less time doing it.

Bastien und Bastienne

Composed when Mozart was all of twelve years old, this seventeen-number German *singspiel* (opera with spoken dialogue between numbers) reveals little if anything of the composer to come. Most of the numbers are extremely short—less than two minutes long—and as the piece only requires three characters, it offers no opportunities for any ensemble larger than the concluding trio. The plot concerns two lovers who consult the village magician to come up with a way to test each other's faithfulness. The story may sound familiar, but even so, *Così fan tutte* this ain't. Really hard-core Mozarteans may want to hear it, and since the entire piece plays for less than an hour, it's certainly a pleasant enough diversion, but nothing more.

La finta semplice (The Fake Simpleton)

This is Mozart's first *opera buffa* (comic opera), and it's no tentative dipping of the toes into the water, but a full-fledged evening of entertainment lasting more than two and a half hours. This fact alone reveals something interesting: namely, that Mozart's later works differ in size from his earlier output (as well as the competition's) more in terms of the proportion of continuous music to recitative than simply by being longer in absolute terms. Indeed, *Semplice* features several numbers in which the recitatives are longer than the already lengthy arias (meaning five or six minutes each), and the longest of the various arias are as long as (or longer than) the finales of the first two acts as well (about seven to eight minutes).

But this should not be of too much concern with a work that was the brainchild of Mozart's father Leopold, who thought it would be a fine idea for his son to prove that a boy of twelve could produce a work as good as the average output of the day. This the young composer certainly accomplished. Originality of conception was very far from both Leopold and Mozart's minds, but as a test of competence, not just in composition but in ability to set the Italian language correctly, *La finta semplice* is a triumph. That it was written at the same time as the wispy and insubstantial *Bastien und Bastienne* is a tribute to one of the preeminent characteristics of Mozart's genius: its adaptability.

This opera also introduces us to a person whose name is useful to know: Italian playwright Carlo Goldoni (1707–1793). Goldoni's plays and librettos were to comic opera what Metastasio's were to *opera seria* (serious opera). They were set literally thousands of times throughout the eighteenth century (and beyond), and many of the stock characters in opera—the misanthropic old man, the clever servant, the young aristocrat in disguise—may be found in his work. One of the more puzzling (to audiences today) aspects of some of Goldoni's librettos concerns the presence of a short third act, which contains the resolution to the complex happenings in the previous two longer ones. In Mozart's later works, the function of this third act is absorbed into the act 2 finale, with literally dramatic results.

Arias to look for:
- "Che scompiglio che flagello"
- "Nelle guerre d'amore"

Mitridate, re di Ponto
Ascanio in Alba
Lucio Silla

These three works belong together, as they were all written for Milan and represent Mozart's only operas specifically intended for performance in Italy. Accordingly, each includes major roles for castratos (now sung by women or countertenors). Early Mozart has been making a comeback lately thanks to the "period performance" movement, and so recordings of the music aren't quite as hard to find as they used to be. You may well find some of the best arias in recitals and on disc. The first of the three Italian operas, *Mitridate,* is a classic opera seria that reads a bit like the later *Idomeneo,* only more so. There's a king who everyone thinks is dead (but he turns out only to be kidding), two guys who want the same woman (instead of two women after the same guy), and the usual conflict between love and duty—all set against an ongoing war between Greece and Rome.

Musically there are some remarkable arias (as is the case in all of these works), including some monstrously long ones loaded with difficult and elaborate ornamentation. Perhaps the best is

Sifare's "Lungi da te, mio bene," with its virtuosic horn solo, but at three hours, the work feels its length. This is less of a problem in *Lucio Silla,* which suffers a bit from a dearth of music for the title character owing to a theoretically inferior singer at the premiere (who still was rewarded with the spectacular sacred motet *Exsultate, jubilate,* K. 165, discussed in the chapter "Sacred Music"), but Mozart's treatment of the orchestra is as imaginative as ever. In particular, he seems to be at pains to reduce the amount of simple recitative, and while this doesn't speed things up especially, it does make listening more interesting. It's worth pointing out that the opera was originally produced with ballet interpolations after each act, although these were not by Mozart. The bottom line: if you enjoy opera seria, then you may well find these works worth sampling.

Arias to look for:

Mitridate
- "Venga pur, minacci e frema"
- "Già dagli occhi il velo è tolto"
- "Va, l'error mio palesa"
- "Lungi da te, mio bene"

Lucio Silla
- "Il tenero momento"
- "Vanne, t'affreta . . . Ah se il crudel periglio"
- "Pupille amate"
- "Quest'improvviso tremito"

Ascanio in Alba is the odd man out in this trio. The work is a *Festa teatrale,* which basically means a one-shot effort composed for a special occasion, in this case, the wedding of the Austrian Archduke Ferdinand to Maria Beatrice d'Este, Princess of Modena. It's sort of the musical equivalent of the paper plates and plastic utensils at a backyard barbeque: perfect for feeding a crowd and conveniently disposable. The story is essentially a two-and-three-quarter-hour-long case of prewedding jitters. Ascanio is nervous about how he will be received by his bride Silvia, a kind and chaste nymph, but Cupid has been sending her dreams of him and she is already in love. His mother, who happens to be Venus (as in the goddess), tells Ascanio not to let Silvia know who he really is, because if he introduced himself normally, the opera would last about two minutes. Again, you may find an aria or two of interest, and the pastoral setting typically calls forth some lovely orchestration, but no one, least of all Mozart, expected this to become a repertory item.

Arias to look for:
- "Dal tuo gentil sembiante"
- "Cara, lontano ancora"
- "Al mio ben mi veggio avanti"

Il sogno de Scipione (Scipio's Dream)

This heavy-duty allegory, to a text by Metastasio, features such thrilling characters as Constancy, Fortune, and License, all of whom engage in a dialogue with Scipio about how to lead a righteous and noble life. The work contains twelve numbers, of which two are choruses, one is an accompanied recitative, and the remainder are arias—really, really long arias, mostly very simply accompanied. Compared to the three Milan operas, *Scipione* is a conservative work of limited range, more oratorio than true opera, but on the plus side, it lasts less than two hours. Mozart wrote it to celebrate the fiftieth anniversary of his patron, the Prince Archbishop of Salzburg, who promptly died before it could be performed. His successor, Hieronimus Colloredo, turned out to be Mozart's nemesis: they hated each other, but it wasn't because the new archbishop disliked *Scipione.* It was first performed (as far as is known) in 1979.

Arias to look for:
- "Lieve son al par del vento"

La finta giardiniera (The Fake Lady Gardener)

This opera is important for several reasons, not the least of which is that is was composed for Munich, as was *Idomeneo* five years later, and the quality of the music reflects well on the high musical standards of that city. You may well ask yourself how it is possible that a mere comedy could last more than three hours: as long as the complete *Idomeneo,* in fact. Maybe it was a Munich thing. Actually, all it takes to answer this question is a brief rundown of the cast of characters:

- Don Anchise, mayor of Lagonero, in love with Sandrina.
- The Marchesa Violanti Onesti, lover of Count Belfiore, believed dead and pretending to be a gardener named Sandrina.
- Count Belfiore, formerly in love with Violanti and now the lover of Arminda.
- Arminda, a Milanese lady, previously in love with Cavaliere Ramiro and now engaged to Count Belfiore.
- Cavaliere Ramiro, in love with Arminda, who has left him.
- Serpetta, the Mayor's maid, in love with him.
- Roberto, Violante's servant, pretending to be her cousin and disguised as a gardener named Nardo, who is in love with Serpetta even though she does not love him.

Now, just how long do you think it should take to sort out this mess? It's possible to even argue, under the circumstances, that *La finta giardiniera* is a marvel of concision (but you won't hear that argument from me). One can even understand the need for the customary short and dramatically questionable third act. Aside from its bizarre length, there's lots of delightful music, and more importantly, the first two acts have extended finales (about fifteen minutes each) that clearly show Mozart moving in the direction of *Figaro*. Indeed, comparing the Da Ponte operas to works such as this, it's very clear that the mature pieces represent a simplification of the typical opera buffa plot scenario. This is what gives Mozart the space he needs to enrich the purely musical element and thus spend the extra time gained on character development. An opera with this story written at *Figaro*'s compositional standard would probably last about a week.

Arias to look for:
- "Geme la tortorella"
- "Crudeli, fermate, crudeli"
- "Ah, dal pianto"
- "Va pure ad altri in braccio"

Il re pastore (The Shepherd King)

Another allegory written for Salzburg with a text by Metastasio, *The Shepherd King* tells the story of Aminta, a shepherd in love with Elisa, whom he has known since childhood. Unbeknown to him, he is the long-lost son of the deposed king of Sidon, which has just been conquered by Alessandro, who does not wish to rule. In fourteen numbers—of which one is the overture, one is the concluding chorus, and the rest are arias—Mozart contrives to get Aminta to accept the kingship and to find a way to marry Elisa despite the fact that she is only a "noble nymph."

This piece represents a big improvement over *Scipio's Dream* in what is, after all, a not-very-promising genre (it's called a

serenata, or *serenade,* which is basically an unstaged mini-opera).
Accordingly the work is short, less than two hours, and might
deserve the occasional concert performance. The most important
and impressive of the arias, Aminta's "L'amerò, sarò costante"
with its lovely violin solo, makes a terrific recital item for an
enterprising soprano with a flair for good, offbeat repertoire.
This is Mozart's last completed operatic work before *Idomeneo,*
and the five years that separate these two pieces represent a world
of difference in his compositional development.

Arias to look for:
- "L'amerò, sarò costante"

Zaide

Mozart worked on *Zaide,* a singspiel for Vienna along the lines
of *The Abduction from the Seraglio,* in 1779, but put it aside when
the commission came for *Idomeneo.* He completed fifteen numbers, or about seventy-five minutes of music. The score includes
one each of chorus, duet, trio, and quartet; ten arias; and two
melodramas—a genre found in no other Mozart operas. This is
simply spoken dialogue accompanied by music, and the melo-
drama at the beginning of act 1 is the longest number in the
work. I have to confess that I detest dialogue in a recording of an
operatic work. It's fine on stage, but I always skip it when listening at home, so the presence of these two numbers here doesn't
thrill me as much as it does Mozart scholars. Still, the music
itself is splendid.

As for the actual story, the libretto is lost, so we don't know
the exact plot, but one can certainly make a very educated guess.
Zaide is the same character as Konstanze, and there's even a servant named Osmin. While the orchestration isn't as colorful as

that which Mozart achieved for *Seraglio,* the music is excellently written and well worth hearing. This appealing torso certainly deserves your attention if you like *Seraglio,* particularly as only a few years separate the two works. Good as *Zaide* is, Mozart's completed Turkish opera takes this popular storyline to another level altogether.

Arias to look for:
- "Ruhe sanft, mein holdes Leben"
- "Tiger! Wetze nur die Klauen"

Der Schauspieldirektor (The Impresario)

This one-act singspiel dates from the same year as *Figaro,* and the music is every bit as good. Mozart composed it at the invitation of the emperor as part of a competition to compare a German singspiel to an Italian opera on the subject of the tribulations of an impresario trying to assemble an opera company out of a temperamental assortment of singers. The composer of the Italian opera was none other than Antonio Salieri, and he won the contest, but then, his music was generally preferred to Mozart's anyway. If there's any problem with *The Impresario,* it's that there is so little of it. In addition to the dialogue, the piece consists of five short numbers, including one of Mozart's very finest overtures (justly famous as a concert piece), followed by an aria, a rondo, a trio, and a concluding vaudeville. The opening two numbers, for the competing sopranos, are both deliciously compact parodies in Mozart's best lovelorn style (prominent clarinets), complete with wacky and extremely flashy, "ready or not, here it comes" flights of *coloratura* (extensive ornamentation and embellishment of the vocal line).

Arias to look for:

- "Da schlägt die Abschiedsstunde"
- "Bester Jüngling!"

Aside from the above works, there are a few other fragments and aborted projects, but nothing of importance. You can see from these brief sketches that the profession of opera composer in Mozart's day was an endless series of compromises. In many ways the work's creator was third in the list of priorities, behind the singers and the librettist. Mozart's early works reflect not so much what he chose to do but rather what he had to do, first to establish his credentials and then to satisfy his patrons. This in turn only serves to increase our admiration for the generally high quality of his work and the near-miraculous excellence of the seven great operas.

Given Mozart's universally acclaimed genius as a composer for the stage, it's easy to understand a certain amount of righteous indignation at the thought of nearly a dozen almost totally neglected works, just as the thrill of discovery and the investment of time and effort involved in getting to know them sometimes leads to overestimation of their worth. It's tempting to claim, as so many do, that "even second-rate Mozart is still better than the best of his contemporaries," particularly when no one knows, cares about, or listens to that music whether good, bad, or indifferent. It's an ironic aspect of Mozart's greatness that not only did his mature work annihilate the music of his colleagues and competitors, it had the same effect on those early works of his that aspire to do little more than imitate them.

Concert Arias

"Alcando, lo confesso . . . Non so d'onde viene,"
   K. 294 (1778)
"No, che non sei capace," K. 419 (1783)
"Ch'io mi scordi di te? . . . Non temer amato bene,"
   K. 505 (1786)
"Bella mia fiamma, addio! . . . Resta, o cara," K. 528
   (1787)
"Giunse alfin il momento . . . Al desio di chi t'adora,"
   K. 577 (1789)
"Schon lacht der holde Frühling," K. 580 (1789)
"Per pieta, non ricercate," K. 420 (1783)
"Mentre ti lascio, oh figlia," K. 513 (1787)
"Un bacio di mano," K. 541 (1788)
"Per questa bella mano," K. 612 (1791)

The loose category in Mozart's catalogue of works that are now called "concert arias" actually consists of three different components:

1. Arias written for insertion into other composer's operas at the request of specific singers
2. Arias written as alternatives for Mozart's own operas
3. Real concert arias, created specifically for vocal recitals

Mozart wrote about fifty pieces that fit one of these three criteria, and they constitute a treasure trove of vocal music that remains comparatively unknown. Chronologically speaking, they date from every period in Mozart's life, from his earliest days as a composer until shortly before his death. Taken together, these arias provide an ideal overview of the art of characterization in music. Indeed, they offer one potential advantage over listening to complete operas, in that you don't have to worry about the broader context and can focus entirely on the relationship between the words and the music in each specific case. They also offer fascinating glimpses into Mozart's private and professional life, and of his relationships with the various singers (some in his own family) that he encountered over the course of his career and the works of other composers whose operas he was called upon to supplement.

I have selected ten of the finest in the series for individual consideration, although there are many more musically rewarding items than space considerations permit me to discuss. Before considering the individual works, let me clarify one technical point. In the arias with double titles separated by ellipsis, the first title refers to the recitative, the second to the aria itself. I provide summary translations of the words in each case.

"Alcando, lo confesso . . . Non so d'onde viene," K. 294 (1778)
2 flutes, 2 clarinets, 2 bassoons, 2 horns, and strings

In 1777, Mozart and his mother spent several months in Mannheim on their way to Paris. The German city was known for its fabulous orchestra, and it was there that Mozart met the two greatest loves of his life: Aloysia Weber, and . . . clarinets (as is known from surviving letters to his father). Aloysia ultimately rejected Mozart—he later married her sister, Constanze—but not before he wrote this aria, his very first piece of vocal or orchestral music scored for the clarinets that ever afterwards remained the instrumental sound of love in his operas. And not just love, but often more specifically, longing. The words are very telling:

[accompanied recitative]
I admit that I am surprised at myself.
His face, his brow, his voice make my
Heart palpitate without warning, and
I feel my blood throbbing in every fiber . . .
[aria]
I don't know from where this tender feeling comes,
This feeling that seems born in my breast,
This ice that runs burning through my veins . . .

One can just imagine how Mozart felt when hearing the object of his desire sing these words to him, as Aloysia did more than once to his delight, to both piano and orchestral accompaniments. Indeed, the aria meant so much to Mozart that he made two versions of it (the opening recitative is the same in both cases), the second even more elaborate, intense, and sensuously scored. Among Aloysia's charms, she was evidently one hell of a singer, and neither her youth (she was about eighteen) nor her inexperience prevented Mozart from writing up to his usual standards or degree of difficulty.

It's always risky to try to connect the meaning of purely musical images to a composer's personal emotions. This is especially true of Mozart, whose compositional logic (as has been seen) when it comes to characterization is not only unsentimentally acute but provocatively honest. However, the inferences drawn here, based on what is known and on that very consistency, are too accurate with respect to Mozart's subsequent practice to be discounted. This aria, Mozart's gift to Aloysia, expresses his yearning for her love, and perhaps the depth and beauty of the similar sentiments found in the ensuing operas would not have taken the form familiar to listeners today had Mozart not met her in Mannheim in 1777 and experienced those feelings himself.

Returning to the music, Mozart was proud of this aria, and rightly so. He told his father that it was the best item in Aloysia's repertoire, sure to gain her applause from audiences everywhere. The melody, with its murmuring accompaniment from strings and winds, perfectly captures the "ice that runs burning" through the singer's veins. A faster and more anxious middle section (the aria is in ABA form) touching on minor keys increases the expressive intensity before the exquisitely prepared return to the opening ideas. The vocal line contains some extremely elaborate runs and plenty of high notes to show off Aloysia's extended top register, but the element of display never sounds gratuitous and never interrupts the long, lyrical line.

One additional point: Mozart set this very same text as a bass aria (K. 512) exactly ten years later, in 1787. Comparison between the two versions is fascinating. The later music is entirely different: more aggressive, aptly masculine, and quicker in tempo, with some brief episodes of very difficult (for a low voice) coloratura in the main body of the aria. It's difficult not to believe that Mozart went out of his way to avoid any trace of resemblance between the two settings, even to the point of having oboes replace the clarinets.

"No, che non sei capace," K. 419 (1783)
2 oboes, 2 horns, 2 trumpets, timpani, and strings

Aloysia did in fact become a successful singer on her move to Vienna and actually took the role of Donna Anna in the Viennese production of *Don Giovanni*. Mozart wrote a total of eight arias for her brilliant coloratura voice, including this thrilling number, featuring trumpets and timpani, that gives the Queen of the Night a good run for her money. Actually, it's both longer and more difficult than either of the Queen's arias in *The Magic Flute*. Mozart composed it as an insertion aria to the opera *Il curioso indescreto* by Pasquale Anfossi (1727–1797), and the text is tailor-made for the big, gutsy musical setting it receives here:

> No, no, no, you aren't capable of courtesy or honor,
> And spout lies in saying that your heart burns for me.
> [in quicker tempo]
> Go away! I hate you, ingrate, and I hate myself even more
> For loving you for even an instant, for sighing over you.

Although much shorter, the contrast in tempos and even the music, particularly in the quicker section, strongly recall "Marten aller Arten" from *The Abduction from the Seraglio* (although there are no extensive instrumental solos as in Konstanze's earlier showpiece). The meaning of both arias is exactly the same: defiance, with the vocal line becoming ever more elaborate as the intensity increases. This would have been a knockout in performance.

"Ch'io mi scordi di te?. . . Non temer amato bene," K. 505 (1786)
2 clarinets, 2 bassoons, 2 horns, piano, and strings

Arguably the finest of all of Mozart's concert arias (or anybody's, for that matter), this number was written for one of his favorite singers, Nancy Storace, for whom he wrote the role of Susanna in *The Marriage of Figaro*. At her farewell concert in Vienna in 1787, she premiered this, Mozart's parting gift to her. Although the words justify the presence of the clarinets, it's the piano that attracts the most attention, with a solo part of concerto-like proportions every bit as important as the vocal line. Mozart played it himself at the concert.

> [recitative]
> That I should forget you?
> You advise me to give myself to him?

And then you want me to live . . . Ah no.
To live thus would be much worse than death . . .
[aria]
Do not fear, my beloved,
My heart forever, forever, will be yours.
I can no longer endure so much pain,
My soul lacks the will to continue . . .

That this is a major work is evident not just in the beauty and finish of the two solo parts but also in the sheer length and variety of texture. The aria lasts nearly ten minutes, making it one of Mozart's largest.

"Bella mia fiamma, addio! . . . Resta, o cara," K. 528 (1787)
flute, 2 oboes, 2 bassoons, 2 horns, and strings

This lovely essay in despair is also a very big piece, about nine minutes long. Mozart wrote it in Prague for his hostess, the singer Josefa Dusek. He had written for her before as early as 1777 ("Ah, lo previdi!," K. 272), and she must have been a graceful and emotionally expressive artist, for this is one of Mozart's darkest pieces, dwelling for the most part in minor keys. It has three big sections: an opening accompanied recitative, a lyrical first half, and a swifter conclusion in which the character looks forward to death.

[accompanied recitative]
Beautiful light of mine, farewell!
It did not please heaven to grant us happiness.
Cut before it could be tied was that pure knot
That united our souls in one will . . .
[aria]
Stay, dear one,

Harsh death separates me—Oh God!—from you.
Take care of her, see that she is comforted.
I go, alas, farewell, farewell, forever . . .
[in quicker tempo]
Ah, where is the temple, where is the altar?
Come, vengeance, hurry!
Oh dear one, farewell, farewell forever.
Ah, a life this bitter cannot be suffered any longer.

One of the most wonderful things about this aria is the transition from the slower tempo to the quicker: so smooth as to be imperceptible, and just enough to get the music moving after its meditative opening. The simultaneous switch to a more cheerful major key at this point should not be seen as contrary to the meaning of the words: at this point the character is looking forward to dying, and affecting a cheerful demeanor.

Also, although written for a soprano, it is obvious from the text that the character singing is male. This is in fact exactly the kind of piece that would have been sung by a castrato in an opera seria. That Mozart did not think anything of making a new setting for female voice strongly indicates not just that castratos were already dying out but that assigning male roles to female singers in conscious imitation of the older tradition was an accepted convention of the day.

"Giunse alfin il momento . . . Al desio di chi t'adora," K. 577 (1789)
2 basset horns, 2 bassoons, 2 horns, and strings

This is called making a virtue out of necessity. Adriana Ferraresi del Bene was Lorenzo Da Ponte's mistress, and the first Fiordiligi in *Così fan tutte*. Judging from this aria, which lies squarely in the middle of the voice for the most part, she was a singer with good flexibility but limited range (exactly the opposite of remarks I have seen concerning her contemporary reputation, in fact). This in turn suggests that "Come scoglio," with its absurd vocal leaps, might have sounded a lot funnier at the premiere of *Così* than it usually does now, when singers try so hard to make beautiful what Mozart clearly intended to sound strained. Ferraresi del Bene demanded two new arias for Susanna when she took on the role in the 1789 revival of *The Marriage of Figaro,* and Mozart, no doubt through gritted teeth, decided that it would be diplomatic to accommodate her.

Believe it or not, this somewhat superficial, flashy, and way-too-long-for-its-dramatic-context aria replaces Susanna's gloriously sensual "Deh vieni" in act 4. As if to save the entire enterprise from going down the musical toilet, Mozart scores the piece with major solos for solo basset horns (low clarinets) and French horns, giving the entire aria a wind serenade–like character and making out of it a sort of Mozartean love music on steroids. It comes close to being a parody, but the orchestration is so gorgeous and interesting in its own right that I have no doubt that the number was resoundingly applauded, to Ferraresi del Bene's complete satisfaction.

The opening recitative is the same one you already know. Only the aria itself is different:

> [accompanied recitative]
> Finally, the hour has come when I will find myself unresistingly
> In the arms of my adored one.
> Timid fears, leave my breast,
> And do not come to disturb my delight . . .
> [aria: note the delicious plucked strings and solo winds when
> the opening line is repeated]
> To the yearning embrace of the one who adores you,
> Come quickly, my beloved!
> I will die if you leave me to sigh

For you longer still . . .
[in quicker tempo]
Ah, I can resist no longer
The passion that inflames my senses.
All those who understand the pangs of love
Will sympathize with me.

This aria demonstrates the lengths to which composers of the day had to go to accommodate the wishes of singers, and let's face it, the singers had a point. People went to operas then, as now, to see the performers, and not because they cared about the composer. A practical man of the theater, Mozart understood that if the singers sounded their best in music proprietarily tailored for them, then at least some of their success would rub off on him, and he would make powerful new friends. The idea of the score being sacrosanct, as we often now insist, would have struck him as crazy, not to mention suicidal from a professional point of view.

"Schon lacht der holde Frühling," K. 580 (1789)
2 clarinets, 2 bassoons, 2 horns, and strings

Aloysia Weber had an older sister, Josepha, who was also a singer with a terrific top and great flexibility. She created the role of the Queen of the Night in *The Magic Flute.* Mozart hated her, not that this is terribly relevant as regards the music he wrote for her to sing (or is it?). This aria was intended to be inserted into a German-language version of Paisiello's *The Barber of Seville* (Rossini was not the first to get his hands on this particular story), but it was never used, so Mozart left some of the orchestration incomplete. There's little doubt as to his intentions, however, and several editors have tidied it up for performance.

The aria is predominantly lively and has a clear ABA form, with the central B section much slower, in a minor key, and beautifully expressive of the text. It displays the yearning quality of Mozart's love music with clarinets to perfection.

> [A section: quick, major key]
> Already beautiful spring is laughing,
> On the flower-dappled meadow,
> Where zephyrs flirt in lively games.
> But although young buds are blooming
> From every branch,
> No sweet comfort resides
> In this poor heart.
> [B section: slow, minor key]
> Here I sit and weep, alone in the meadow,
> Not for my lost little lamb, but for Lindor, the shepherd.
> [A section modified and repeated]

Listening to the very special and virtuosic music that Mozart wrote for Josepha and her sister Aloysia only highlights the extent to which his art was inspired by the specific abilities of the musicians in his immediate circle of friends and family, and the remarkable community of exceptional Viennese vocal and instrumental performers that served him so well.

"Per pieta, non ricercate," K. 420 (1783)
2 clarinets, 2 bassoons, 2 horns, and strings

This piece, for tenor, is another insertion aria for Pasquale Anfossi's *Il curioso indescreto,* and there is one more besides (K. 418, for soprano). Indeed, one can only wonder in cases such as this if what was eventually performed deserved to list the original composer at all. Note the orchestration: this is Mozart's typical love music scoring, although the words are generic and give no indication as to the specifics of the situation. As I noted previously, one needs to take care not to underestimate Mozart's inspiration or flexibility in adapting his accompaniments to many different moods and emotions.

> For pity's sake, do not look for an explanation for my torment;
> I feel it so cruelly that I can't explain it . . .
> [quicker tempo]
> Ah, between anger and between indignation at my dreary
> situation,
> I only call, oh God, on death to come and comfort me.

This aria is a rondo—that is, it has a two-tempo, slow–fast form. The woodwinds are very prominent, particularly in the quicker section when, at the words "I only call, oh God, on death," the tempo slows down once again for a stunning mingling of tenor voice and clarinet tone. There are only eight concert arias for tenor, none more beautiful or voluptuous sounding than this.

"Mentre ti lascio, oh figlia," K. 513 (1787)
flute, 2 clarinets, 2 bassoons, 2 horns, strings

The world of opera tends to focus so much on sopranos and tenors that it sometimes seems surprising that other vocal types get any consideration at all. The predominance of sopranos, particularly in earlier music, is easy to understand, since this includes castratos and therefore men. In fact, Mozart also wrote eight arias for bass/baritone, and this is one of the largest of them, lasting about eight minutes in performance. The scoring beautifully underlines the heartbreak of parting expressed in the text:

> While I leave you, o daughter, my heart trembles.
> Alas, what bitter parting!

My sadness brings both anguish and terror.
I go. You weep? Oh God!
I ask but a moment, Oh God, what fearful torment!
Ah, my heart is breaking!

Because the text is short, there's a great deal of word repetition. The first time through, broken rhythms, a dark minor key, and chromatic harmony give the impression of a funeral march, but Mozart has a surprise in store. The tempo begins to accelerate and the music gains in energy. The harmony shifts to the major, and the ending is strangely positive for such a despairing message. Is this heroic resolve to put the best face on a terrible situation, despite the initial expression of despair, or is Mozart acceding to the demands of a particular singer? You be the judge.

"Un bacio di mano," K. 541 (1788)
flute, 2 oboes, 2 bassoons, 2 horns, and strings

In the first volume of this guide, devoted to Mozart's instrumental music, I included this little two-minute comic aria for baritone on that book's CD for two reasons. First, many people buy recordings of the "Jupiter" Symphony (No. 41) and are told that the second subject of its first movement comes from this aria. Naturally this arouses curiosity, but who wants to have to hunt around and buy an entire CD to hear about 50 percent of a two-minute aria?

Second, much of that first volume concerns the vocal origins of Mozart's instrumental style, and his treatment of the tune from this aria perfectly illustrates how he intensifies the original expressive intent of the vocal melody when he gives it to instruments alone. The comparison is still a useful one, and so if this issue piques your interest and you wish to continue your exploration of Mozart with his instrumental works (assuming that you haven't already sampled them extensively), then I offer this shameless plug for volume 1 as a means of whetting your appetite.

> A kiss on the hand
> Will accomplish wonders for you.
> And now, lovely girl
> You are ready to get married . . .
> You're a little foolish,
> My dear Pompeo.
> Go out and study
> The ways of the world.

Perhaps the most charming aspect of this aria lies not in the tune that Mozart reused in the symphony but in the delicious march that so succinctly illustrates the idea of "going out" to study the ways of the world. It may be short, but it really is a toe-tapper of a piece.

"Per questa bella mano," K. 612 (1791)
flute, 2 oboes, 2 bassoons, 2 horns, double bass solo, and strings

We are justified in taking Mozart seriously, but not if this leads us to forget just how funny he can be, and so, after so much music evocative of yearning, despair, and suffering, I'd like to conclude with a bit of pure fun. Mozart wrote this wacky aria for the same bass who shortly afterwards took the utterly humorless role of Sarastro at the premiere of *The Magic Flute*. The combination of this voice type with solo double bass guarantees that however sincere the singer's protestations of love, the rug is constantly being pulled out from under him.

By this beautiful hand, by these gentle glances, I swear,
    my dear,
That I shall never love anyone but you.
The breezes, the plants, the rocks who know my sighing
    so well,
Will tell you about my constant faithfulness.
Whether your glances are sympathetic or proud,
Whether you say that you hate or love me,
I am constantly pierced by sweet darts of love,
And always ask that you call me yours.
Never changing, not by earth or heaven,
Is this desire that lives in me.

This aria is also a rondo, first slow then fast. The slow section has the marked rhythm of a country dance or crude waltz, and the wind interjections make it sound even more like a calliope or merry-go-round at a country fair. The music actually sounds fat—really there's no better way to describe it. The quick section sends the double bass scrambling to make its presence felt, and when the singer hits the last line, describing his never-changing desire, one finds the same extreme, and extremely amusing, vocal leaps that undermine the determination of Fiordiligi in her similarly unsteady protestation of undying fidelity, "Come scoglio," from *Così fan tutte.*

So this aria provides some genuine merriment, but it also reveals something important: that Mozart's musical language operates by way of a consistently used expressive vocabulary of gestures, motives, melodic shapes, and instrumental sounds. Hearing these isolated arias doesn't provide an exhaustive survey of Mozart's style in this respect, but they remind listeners, in this day and age of scholarly correctness and a positive fetish for completeness at all costs, that Mozart would have thought it perfectly normal and reasonable for you to take in a favorite aria or two if you didn't have time for the whole opera. You could certainly do far worse then to spend some time with any of these gems, or the numerous other members of this particularly appealing family—one that in so many ways represents the essence of Mozart's art of writing for the voice.

Sacred Music

Exsultate, jubilate, K. 165 (1773)
Missa Brevis in F, K. 192 (1774)
"Coronation" Mass in C Major, K. 317 (1779)
Vesperae solennes de confessore, K. 339 (1780)
Mass in C Minor, K. 427 (1782–83) and Davidde pen-
itente, K. 469 (1785)
Ave Verum Corpus, K. 618 (1791)
Requiem, K. 626 (1791)

It's probably fair to say that Mozart disliked writing sacred music, at least for the most part. Of the approximately twenty Masses and Mass movements, seven liturgies and services, twenty-five miscellaneous short pieces, and a smattering of oratorios and sacred cantatas, no other body of his music can claim such a high proportion of perfunctory, just plain uninteresting work. There are several reasons for this, the first being that composing for the church was his primary job in Salzburg when he was either very young or in the service of Archbishop Heironimus Colloredo. The two loathed each other, and under the circumstances, writing liturgical music was for Mozart quite literally a penance.

The second reason stems from the simple fact that Mozart was above all a composer for the theater with an inherent flair for the dramatic, and sacred music makes a point of being spiritual, which essentially means antitheatrical. While music for the stage seeks to convey the impression of continuous forward movement at a natural human pace, religious music wants to achieve a sense of timelessness on a more than merely human scale. This aversion to theatricality largely accounts for the conservatism of most liturgical music, its reliance on age-old forms and procedures.

Only one great composer in Mozart's day succeeded in reconciling the demands of the Catholic liturgy with the latest stylistic developments of the classical period, and that was Joseph Haydn, whose unselfconscious blending of the baroque contrapuntal style with genuine symphonic development created a new type of religious music as surely as Mozart's mixture of opera seria and opera buffa birthed a new dramatic medium on the stage. At the time of his death, Mozart was definitely heading towards a musical idiom that could have achieved a similar synthesis, and it's our loss that what would undoubtedly have been his two greatest sacred pieces, the Mass in C Minor and the Requiem, were both left incomplete, although for different reasons.

The C Minor Mass is the critical work in this respect. It remained unfinished simply because Mozart quit, leaving unsettled the two biggest problems that anyone setting this text has to deal with. The first of these is the fact that the final section, the Agnus Dei/Dona Nobis Pacem, invariably creates an anticlimax if composers wish to make their music reflect the intent of the words ("Lamb of God who takes away the sins of the world, grant us peace"). The Mass accordingly must conclude peacefully, and while Mozart had no problem with tranquil endings, the text alone affords no opportunity to organically justify such an ending after all that has come before. Both Haydn and Beethoven, for example, got around this dilemma by going beyond the strict scope of the words, contrasting the trumpets and drums of the Napoleonic Wars with the liturgical prayer for divine solace.

However Mozart's art, as discussed, was probably the most nonillustrative of any great composer's. His brilliance as a writer of vocal music principally lay in finding the perfect musical equivalent to the emotional sense of the text. Certainly he could have conceived of such a solution had he wanted to, but his mind simply didn't work that way. In *Idomeneo,* for example, I noted how the storm chorus emerged from Elettra's inner turmoil, from the human conflict, and not the other way around. For Mozart, expressing human emotion in music was his calling, and it is surely significant in the C Minor Mass that the Credo breaks off in midstream, after the Et Incarnatus at the words "and was made *man.*" As you will see, in his best sacred music, whenever the text suggests some opportunity for the expression of feelings, Mozart seizes it with relish, but elsewhere he betrays not a shred of sympathy for, or interest in, the purely spiritual or theological aspects of religious texts.

I've seen it said in discussions of *The Magic Flute* that Mozart's finest liturgical music consists of the scenes in Sarastro's temple, where he was inspired by the idea of a philosophy dedicated to brotherhood and enlightenment. Elsewhere, in most of his music for the church, Mozart contented himself (and doubtless his audience) with a generalized prettiness that was guaranteed to get the job done with a minimum of fuss and bother, offending no one. He was more than qualified in this respect, but the results are not great Mozart, and there's no shame in admitting the fact that even a genius did not or could not do everything equally well. The following seven works comprise the most popular and/or highly regarded pieces of sacred music that Mozart composed, the ones you will most likely encounter in concert performance and on recordings.

Exsultate, jubilate, K. 165
2 oboes, 2 horns, and strings (with organ continuo)

Mozart wrote this brilliant "motet" in Milan for the same castrato (Venanzio Rauzzini) who had just sung the title role in the premiere of *Lucio Silla*. I put the word *motet* in quotation marks because other than signifying a short sacred work, the term has been applied historically to the widest range of styles and forms. What we have here is a concert aria, plain and simple, similar to Bach's Cantata No. 51 for solo soprano, *Jauchzet Gott in allen Landen*. The mood is entirely joyous, with theatrical displays of coloratura heightening the emotion.

The work, which lasts about fifteen minutes, has four sections:

Allegro [full orchestra]:
Rejoice, shout, O you blessed souls, singing sweet hymns;
The skies sing psalms with me, in reply to your songs.
Recitative:
Friendly daylight glows, both storms and clouds have passed,
An unexpected calm has arrived for the righteous . . .
Andante [strings]:
Grant us peace, you crown of virgins.
You, ready to offer consolation wherever a heart sighs.
Allegro [full orchestra]:
Alleluia.

If you enjoy Mozart's concert arias, you will certainly love this piece. It shows that even at such a young age, he not only had skill but a melodic fluency and natural sense of timing that simply cannot be taught. When listening, you may well find that the music has ended before you know it. The time flies by effortlessly. If there is such a thing as religious entertainment, then this is it.

Missa Brevis in F, K. 192
2 violins, bass, organ (optional trombones and trumpets), soloists and choir (both soprano/alto/tenor/bass [SATB])

This charming piece is typical of Mozart's settings of the *Missa Brevis* (or short Mass), scored for limited forces and designed to get the whole service over with as quickly as possible. The scoring for these pieces was, of necessity, flexible. Only the strings are essential, and they can be played as solos or by any larger number, depending on what's available. Similarly, the bass line could employ any combination of low strings and winds plus the organ, which plays an old-fashioned continuo part with a figured bass (meaning the accompanying chords for organ are written in a sort of musical shorthand and improvised on the spot). So instrumental color is almost never a factor in works of this type, and this already means that Mozart is working in pastels, musically speaking, rather than oils.

The reason this Mass has become popular stems from the fact that its Credo quotes the same four-note motive that would later launch the finale of the "Jupiter" Symphony (No. 41), which is very amusing when you consider that the first movement's second subject is a tune from the buffo aria "Un bacio di mano," as mentioned in the previous chapter. The truth is that this little motive is one of the commonplace elements of the musical language of Mozart's day. It figures just as prominently in the finale of Haydn's very early Symphony No. 13, and the finale of the same composer's "Drumroll" Symphony (No. 103) employs a slightly different motive, but the concept is very similar. As you will shortly see, this Credo is remarkable in a number of other ways as well.

All Mass settings, whether by Mozart or his contemporaries, employ to some extent a consistent descriptive language suggested by the text, tradition, and what the church considered permissible, and this work gives a good sense of how that language operates. In terms of vocal forces, the choir alternates with brief passages for soloists, who in Mozart's day would have been drawn from the ranks of the choristers. This offers some opportunity for contrast, particularly in the longest movements, the Gloria and the Credo. Otherwise, there are no specific rules as to what lines go to the soloists and which go to the full choir.

Kyrie

There is absolutely nothing about this setting that suggests any attempt to put some emotional force behind the plea "Lord have mercy." It's simply amiable music that bounces along without a care in the world. The central section, "Christ have mercy," is here set to the same tunes, although in larger settings it often becomes an independent movement. Since the entire text consists only of six words—*Kyrie eleison, Christe eleison, Kyrie eleison*—the tradition is to stretch them out through much repetition. Mozart keeps them rolling along for about three and a half minutes.

Gloria

The opening line, "Gloria in excelsis Deo" (Glory to God in the highest), was often sung in the form of chant, so Mozart begins the Gloria with the next clause: "Et in terra pax" (And on earth peace). This music returns between the later clauses, set to different words, as a kind of refrain, making the movement a freely organized rondo. Different from the slow–fast "aria version" of the rondo, this kind has the form ABACA, etc. Mozart creates an expressive, aptly minor-key middle section at "Qui tollis paccata mundi, miserere nobis" (Thou who takest away the sins of the world, have mercy on us). The Gloria traditionally ends with a fugue on the final clause. Mozart doesn't have room for one in such a compact setting, and so he brings in each voice successively, as though beginning a fugue, before moving on directly to the concluding "amen" without further elaboration. The entire movement lasts about five minutes.

Credo

Mozart decides to make some mischief in this movement, the longest and most difficult text because of its lengthy recitation of doctrinal clauses, and this fact alone speaks volumes about his attitude towards compositional work that he probably regarded as drudgery. The opening, as noted, consists of the four-note "Jupiter" Symphony theme, and as in the Gloria, the music (and this time, the same words) returns throughout the movement as a refrain. Mozart does pay his respects to the obligatory word painting: the Crucifixus is properly subdued, and there are sudden drops in tempo and volume when the subject of death comes up. But what is one to make of the following oddities?

1. At the words "descendit de coelis" (descended from heaven), almost every Mass setting in the universe has descending musical lines. Mozart sets the word *descendit* to a falling interval, but the vocal parts rises in four successively higher leaps.
2. Similarly, after the Resurrection, when Christ ascends to heaven (*et ascendit*), Mozart does exactly the same thing: the word takes in a rising interval, but the vocal line falls in four sequential entries, beginning with the sopranos and ending with the basses, going down.
3. The assertion in the belief of one holy Catholic and Apostolic Church makes an excellent opportunity for a strong unison melody. Mozart deliberately repeats the word *unam* (one) three times in a row (the Trinity?), but more to the point,

the sopranos are quite intentionally out of whack, beginning the otherwise unison phrase before everyone else and taking a couple of bars to catch up.

Speculation about a composer's motives can never be more than that: mere guesswork, but there's definitely something curious going on here, and one can easily imagine Mozart and his friends having a little six-minute-long chuckle at the Archbishop's expense in this half-solemn, half-joking Credo.

Sanctus/Osanna
Benedictus/Osanna

Each of these movements lasts less than two minutes. The Sanctus is a tiny choral hymn, while the Osanna is cheerful little fugue. Soloists begin the Benedictus (also a frequent occurrence in Mass settings), which concludes traditionally with the same Osanna.

Agnus Dei/Dona Nobis Pacem

The expressive heart of this Mass, the Agnus is one of those heartfelt minor-key choral laments that will culminate in the Lacrimosa of the Requiem (CD tracks 17 and 19). Mozart switches to the major mode for the pastoral setting of Dona Nobis Pacem. The rhythm, which is the compound meter 6/8, is exactly the same as that used to characterize peasants and servants such as Zerlina in *Don Giovanni* or Despina in *Così fan tutte,* and it gives the music a dancelike, open-air quality that brings the Mass to the necessary peaceful close.

This Missa Brevis illustrates perfectly the mixture of the bland and the characterful that typifies so much of Mozart's sacred music. It also highlights how difficult it is for any composer to achieve originality of expression while respecting longstanding musical practice and setting the same words over and over, particularly in this restrictive format.

"Coronation" Mass in C Major, K. 317

2 oboes, 2 horns, 2 trumpets, timpani, organ continuo, three trombones (doubling the alto, tenor, and bass chorus parts throughout), strings (violins, cellos, and basses), soloists and choir (both SATB)

Despite its grandeur and far more massive sonority, this piece too qualifies as a Missa Brevis to the extent that it's only about six or seven minutes longer than K. 192, which lasts about twenty. This is if anything an even cooler work, emotionally speaking. It has one expressively gripping moment: the Et Incarnatus Est/ Cucifixus section of the Credo, which is set in a slower tempo and contrasting minor key. Otherwise, the useful point this music makes is that often in these situations, the setting reflects not the text being sung but the occasion for which the work was composed. That's certainly the case here, and so like *Exsultate, jubilate,* this Mass falls squarely into the category of "religious entertainment."

What makes this music especially appealing is the well-timed alternation between chorus and soloists, very deftly handled (especially in the opening Kyrie), as well as the subtle way that Mozart deploys his brass and percussion. From the very first bars, you will note the contrast between loud outbursts from the orchestra followed by a quiet response from the choir, which gives the work grandeur as well as a certain depth of calm appropriate for a solemn religious ceremony. Much of the music has a majestic, processional character as well. The Benedictus, however, given to the soloists as previously, is a pure opera buffa andante, with a charming melody that can't help but raise a smile. Also interesting is the near total absence of counterpoint: there are no fugues at the ends of the Gloria or Credo, and after a peaceful opening, Mozart concludes the Dona Nobis Pacem with plenty of fanfare in the brass and timpani.

It used to be thought that the nickname originated in the work's having been composed for the annual coronation ritual of a statue of the Virgin Mary in a Salzburg church, but apparently the work may have been used in an actual coronation ceremony in Vienna in around 1790. Whatever the reason, the name certainly fits this stately piece, which makes a much bigger impression than its size and length would at first suggest.

Vesperae solennes de confessore, K. 339

2 trumpets, optional trombones, timpani, bass (a mixture of cellos, basses, and bassoon), strings, organ, soloists and choir (both SATB)

On Sundays and feast days in Salzburg, two services were generally held: High Mass in the morning and a Vespers service in the afternoon. Mozart wrote two Vespers settings, of which this is the best known (the other is the *Vesperae de Dominica*, K. 321), but both contain beautiful music. The service itself consists of a sequence of five psalms and concludes with the Magnificant, the exultant prayer of the Virgin Mary (from the Gospel of Luke) on learning that she is to be the mother of Jesus Christ. Here is the precise order:

- Dixit Dominus (Psalm 110)
- Confitebor (Psalm 11)
- Beatus Vir (Psalm 112)
- Laudate Pueri (Psalm 113)

- Laudate Dominum (Psalm 117)
- Magnificat (Luke 1: 46–55)

Each section then ends with the same formula: "Gloria to the Father, the Son, and to the Holy Spirit. As it was in the beginning, so shall it be forever, world without end, Amen."

The work is beautifully proportioned, each movement lasting around four to five minutes, resulting in a very enjoyable and well-contrasted half hour of music. Again Mozart is mindful of the intended context, and this means an avoidance of extremes of emotional contrast, but the colorful verbal imagery of the Psalms gives him much greater latitude in word setting. In practice, this means a lively interchange between the choir and soloists, often accompanied by distinctive harmonic shadings (such as the lovely minor-key digression in Beatus Vir at the words "The righteous man will be remembered forever. He will not fear evil tidings").

Laudate Pueri is particularly impressive, set entirely in a stern minor key and followed by the strongest possible contrast in the form of the gracious, consoling Laudate Dominum, exquisitely arranged for solo soprano and choir. The entry of the massed voices after the lengthy opening solo is truly magical, with hauntingly beautiful harmony. It's a great Mozart moment by any standard, as is the way the soprano voice returns with the final "amen," rising out of the choral mass like a beam of sunlight breaking through the clouds. After a grand opening, the concluding Magnificat takes off with plenty of joyous trumpeting and drumming, and particularly effective solos for the female soloists (this is, after all, the Virgin Mary speaking).

All told, this work offers the best of Mozart's Salzburg church music: engaging, tuneful but never trivial, and full of beautiful ideas succinctly realized.

Mass in C Minor, K. 427

flute, 2 oboes, 2 bassoons, 2 horns, 2 trumpets,
3 trombones, timpani, strings, organ, 2 sopranos, tenor,
bass, 8-part choir (SSAATTBB)

Davidde penitente, K. 469

2 flutes, 2 oboes, 2 clarinets, 2 bassoons, 2
horns, 2 trumpets, 3 trombones, timpani, strings, organ,
2 sopranos, tenor, 4-part choir (SATB)

I put these two works together because they are the same piece, more or less. The C Minor Mass, universally acclaimed as Mozart's greatest sacred work, consists of a complete Kyrie and Gloria, a tiny fragment of a Credo, a brief Sanctus and Osanna, and a Benedictus. It is (or would have been) what's known as a *cantata Mass*, a form often employed in larger settings, wherein the various texts are broken up into arias, ensembles, and choruses as in an opera or oratorio. Bach's B Minor Mass is the most famous example of this genre. Indeed, oratorio was very much on Mozart's mind; he had been recently busy arranging Handel (including his *Messiah*) for more modern instrumental forces, and the big choruses in this Mass have a very Handelian grandeur and power, as you can hear for yourself on the accompanying CD (track 20), which offers the conclusion of the very glorious Gloria. The text is simply: "Jesus Christ, with the Holy Spirit, in the glory of God the Father, Amen."

A few years after laying aside the Mass, Mozart needed to cobble together a new oratorio for performance in Vienna, and so, with the help of Da Ponte, he took the music of the Mass and simply added new Italian words over the existing Latin ones, adding in the process two arias, a bit for the trio of soloists in the final chorus, and clarinets. The beauty of the soprano writing in both works is particularly noteworthy (one of the parts was intended for his wife, Constanze, and I already mentioned how accomplished the Weber sisters were as vocalists): check out the Laudamus Te and its Italian equivalent, which are pure opera. Even if you don't speak Latin or Italian, you can also see that the new words often follow the sense of the old (for example, the Gloria), and it's certainly no accident that Mozart chose "The Penitent David" as the subject for an oratorio that begins with his most moving, minor-key setting of the Kyrie, truly a passionate plea for mercy.

Rather than dwell on the two works in further detail, I offer below a table that describes their relationship to one another; you might enjoy comparing them on your own.

Mass	Oratorio
Kyrie	Alzai le flebili voci al Signor
Gloria In Excelsis Deo	Cantiam le glorie
Laudamus Te	Lungi le cure ingrate
Gratias	Sii pur sempre benigno, Oh Dio
Domine Deus	Sorgi, O Signore
New Aria:	A te, fra tanti affanni
Qui Tollis Peccata Mundi	Se vuoi puniscimi
New Aria:	Tra l'oscure ombre funeste
Quoniam Tu Solus Sanctus	Tutte le mie speranze
Jesu Christe—Cum Sancto Spiritu	Chi in Dio sol spera—Di tai pericoli non ha timor

Ave Verum Corpus, K. 618
strings, organ, and chorus (SATB)

This exquisite little prayer, less than four minutes long, expresses the following text in a single, flowing paragraph full of elegiac serenity:

Hail true body, born of the Virgin Mary, truly tortured and sacrificed on the cross for mankind. From whose pierced side water and blood flow, you shall be our nourishment when death tests us.

Stylistically, the piece recalls the style of the temple scenes in *The Magic Flute,* and it also was adapted for instruments alone by Tchaikovsky, as the slow movement in his Fourth Orchestral Suite "Mozartiana." It's just unbelievably beautiful, period.

Requiem, K. 626
2 basset horns, 2 bassoons, 2 trumpets, 3 trombones, timpani, organ, strings, soloists (SATB) and choir (SATB)

It's singularly ironic, given the amount of great music that Mozart left, that perhaps his most popular choral piece was not only unfinished but completed by others. Of the Requiem's fourteen movements, the first ten have at least vocal parts, a bass line, and perhaps some indications of orchestration by Mozart. The last four (Sanctus, Benedictus, Agnus Dei, and Communio) were composed entirely by his pupil Franz Xaver Süssmayer, who also filled in the details of the first ten as necessary (the opening Requiem and Kyrie seem to have been virtually complete). Ever since then, various editions have appeared correcting Süssmayer, incorporating newly discovered sketches and otherwise tinkering to the point where an entire Mozart Requiem industry has built up around the piece.

This, combined with the romantic story of its creation (anonymously commissioned by Count Walsegg-Stuppach so he could pass it off as his own work) and Mozart's serendipitous death have exercised an irresistible hold on the public's imagination ever since. Because the movements are all short, the scoring modest, and the choral writing comparatively easy, the piece is also a sure-fire hit with amateur choral societies and community orchestras. Finally, the unimpressive quality of so much of Mozart's other choral and liturgical music throws the deeply expressive music of the Requiem into high relief, making it a pretty safe assumption that it would have been a very great work indeed had he lived to complete it.

Unfortunately Mozart did not live to complete it, and despite the best efforts of everyone involved, it remains a fragmentary, spasmodic work full of beautiful ideas that often seem insufficiently worked out, judging by the standards of Mozart's greatest music. It also may come as shock on seeing the manuscript to note that the unidiomatic, ornately bel canto trombone solo opening the Tuba Miram (theoretically the trumpet of the apocalypse) was actually not Süssmayer's but Mozart's. Never mind. It's not my purpose to suggest that anyone should or should not like music so obviously rich in feeling. I simply want to emphasize that one's experience of Mozart's vocal music should not be based on "the story behind the work" (however juicy) and centered on this single piece to the exclusion of other, indisputably great, complete ones.

My real reason for concluding this chapter, and also this book, with the Requiem (aside from chronology) is that it presents an opportunity to consider one of the most important recent happenings in the history of classical music performance, and so to end with two different views of the sound of Mozart's music in your ears. On the accompanying CD, tracks 16 through 19, you will find two performances of the Confutatis and Lacrimosa movements, one played traditionally on modern instruments and the other performed according to the most recent research into period instrument construction, singing, and playing. Here are the two texts:

Confutatis

[men only, with trumpets and drums and agitated strings]

Confutatis maledictis,	When the damned are silenced,
Flammis acribus addictis,	And given to the intense flames,

[women, gently, alternating with the above]

Voca me cum benedictis.	Call me among the blessed.

[full chorus, beseeching]

Oro supplex et acclinis,	I pray, kneeling in supplication,
Cor contritum quasi cinis:	With a heart contrite as ashes:
Gere curam mei finis.	Take my end into Thy care.

Lacrimosa

[full chorus, with two-note, sobbing figures on the violins]

Lacrimosa dies illa,	On that day of weeping,
Qua resurget ex favilla,	From the ashes will arise
Judicandus homo reus.	The guilty, to be judged.
Huic ergo parce, Deus.	Therefore, spare this one, Lord.
Pie Jesu domine:	Merciful Lord Jesus:
Dona eis requiem.	Grant them rest.
Amen.	Amen.

The first difference that you will notice is one of tempo: the HIP (Historically Informed Practice) rendition (tracks 18 and 19) is much quicker. This gives the Confutatis greater urgency and produces a gently elegiac Lacrimosa. The traditional performance (tracks 16 and 17) has a softer edge in the Confutatis, but the Lacrimosa sounds darker and significantly more tragic in tone. Smaller forces in the HIP version permit greater clarity of rhythm, with more cut to the sound of trumpets and drums as compared to the pronounced massiveness and dignity of the full symphony orchestra and large chorus. Certainly this is the same music, with the same general emotional tone, but otherwise the contrasts are very telling, and preference for one style over the other must remain a matter of personal taste. Personally, I like the more vicious Confutatis and the slower, sadder Lacrimosa, and you should feel free to mix and match similarly.

The HIP movement, which really hit its stride just in time for the 200th anniversary of Mozart's death in 1991, brought new life and urgency to performances of music that everyone thought they knew almost to death. It revealed a universe of color and drama, even in sacred music, that had sometimes gotten lost in the huge spaces of modern concert halls, and was further smothered by the training of today's orchestral musicians in the rather condescending nineteenth-century attitude that music of the classical period requires handling with kid gloves. These so-called authentic performances, with their smaller forces, sometimes creaky instruments, and (at the movement's inception) often alarmingly ugly sounds, put the danger and virtuosity back into this music, and no one benefited more than did Mozart.

Then the reaction set in, and indeed continues to this day. Modern players now often take note of the swifter tempos, the instrumental transparency, and the rhythmic acuity, and modify their interpretations accordingly while retaining the smooth timbres and warm tonal qualities that listeners so enjoy today in symphonic music. A whole new generation of singers, smaller of voice (as in Mozart's day) than audiences had previously come to expect, and wonderfully supple, virtuosic, and able to ornament the vocal line idiomatically, have made listening to a Mozart opera or vocal work one of the best bets in the world of music when it comes to quality of performance.

Most importantly, this flurry of activity, both live and on recordings, has reaffirmed the very traditional notion of what it means to be a "classic": that the music is bigger than any one performance, and that it has more to offer than any single interpretation (or book) can convey. It therefore rewards repetition, and as much time as you have to give it. Mozart, for all the talk about his music's very real and powerful expressivity and depth of emotion, is not an easy composer to pin down, precisely because he is so rich, so subtle, so damn *pretty*, and therefore so multifaceted. But that is also why generations of performers and listeners return to him with pleasure and always find something new, and moving, and beautiful.

CD Track Listing

1. Cavatina: "Porgi, amor" from *Le nozze di Figaro* (3:40)
   Sir Charles Mackerras, conductor, Scottish Chamber Orchestra
   Carol Vaness
   From Telarc CD-80388

2. Overture from *Così fan tutte* (4:03)
   Sir Charles Mackerras, conductor, Scottish Chamber Orchestra
   From Telarc CD-80360

3. Terzetto: "La mia Dorabella capace non è" from *Così fan tutte* (1:48)
   Sir Charles Mackerras, conductor, Scottish Chamber Orchestra
   Jerry Hadley, Asessandro Corbelli, Gilles Cachemaille
   From Telarc CD-80360

4. Recitativo: "Fuor la spada!" from *Così fan tutte* (1:11)
   Sir Charles Mackerras, conductor, Scottish Chamber Orchestra
   Jerry Hadley, Asessandro Corbelli, Gilles Cachemaille
   From Telarc CD-80360

5. Terzetto: "È la fede delle femmine" from *Così fan tutte* (1:11)
   Sir Charles Mackerras, conductor, Scottish Chamber Orchestra
   Jerry Hadley, Asessandro Corbelli, Gilles Cachemaille
   From Telarc CD-80360

6. Recitativo: "Scioc#cherie di poeti!" from *Così fan tutte* (1:31)
   Sir Charles Mackerras, conductor, Scottish Chamber Orchestra
   Jerry Hadley, Asessandro Corbelli, Gilles Cachemaille
   From Telarc CD-80360

7. Terzetto: "Una bella serenata" from *Così fan tutte* (2:18)
   Sir Charles Mackerras, conductor, Scottish Chamber Orchestra
   Jerry Hadley, Asessandro Corbelli, Gilles Cachemaille
   From Telarc CD-80360

8. Finale: "Esci omai" from *Le nozze di Figaro* (19:08)
   Sir Charles Mackerras, conductor, Scottish Chamber Orchestra and Chorus
   Alessandro Corbelli, Carol Vaness, Nuccia Focile, Alastair Miles, Alfonso Antoniozzi,
   Suzanne Murphy, Ryland Davies
   From Telarc CD-80388

9. Chorus: "Singt dem großen Bassa Lieder" from *Die Entführung aus dem
   Serail* (1:40)
   Sir Charles Mackerras, conductor, Scottish Chamber Orchestra and Chorus
   From Telarc CD-80544

10. Aria: "Non più andrai" from *Le nozze di Figaro* (3:45)
    Sir Charles Mackerras, conductor, Scottish Chamber Orchestra
    Alastair Miles
    From Telarc CD-80388

11. Aria: "Madamina, il catalogo è questo" from *Don Giovanni* (5:33)
Sir Charles Mackerras, conductor, Scottish Chamber Orchestra
Alessandro Corbelli
From Telarc CD-80420

12. Aria: "Mi tradì quell'alma ingrate" from *Don Giovanni* (3:48)
Sir Charles Mackerras, conductor, Scottish Chamber Orchestra
Felicity Lott
From Telarc CD-80420

13. Aria: "Dalla sua pace" from *Don Giovanni* (4:04)
Sir Charles Mackerras, conductor, Scottish Chamber Orchestra
Jerry Hadley
From Telarc CD-80420

14. Aria: "Come scoglio immoto resta" from *Così fan tutte* (4:40)
Sir Charles Mackerras, conductor, Scottish Chamber Orchestra
Feliciy Lott
From Telarc CD-80360

15. Aria: "Die Hölle Rache kocht in meinem Herzen" from *Die Zauberflöte* (3:02)
Sir Charles Mackerras, conductor, Scottish Chamber Orchestra
June Anderson
From Telarc CD-80302

16. Requiem, K. 626: Confutatis (2:32)
Robert Shaw, conductor, Atlanta Symphony Orchestra and Chorus
From Telarc CD-80128

17. Requiem, K. 626: Lacrimosa (3:28)
Robert Shaw, conductor, Atlanta Symphony Orchestra and Chorus
From Telarc CD-80128

18. Requiem, K. 626: Confutatis (2:02)
New completion by Robert Levin
Martin Pearlman, director, Boston Baroque
From Telarc CD-80410

19. Requiem, K. 626: Lacrimosa (2:38)
New completion by Robert Levin
Martin Pearlman, director, Boston Baroque
From Telarc CD-80410

20. Mass in C Minor, K. 427: Jesu Christe/Cum Sancto (5:01)
Robert Shaw, conductor, Atlanta Symphony Orchestra and Chorus
From Telarc CD-80150